Ofari, Earl.
   Let your motto be resistance; the life and thought of Henry
Highland Garnet.   Boston, Beacon Press [1972]

   xi, 221 p.   21 cm. $7.95

   "Selected speeches and writings of Henry Highland Garnet": p. [127]-203.
Bibliography: p. [213]-215.

   1. Garnet, Henry Highland, 1815-1882.   2. United States—Race questions.
I. Title.

E449.G214O33   1972   323.4'092'4   72-75543
ISBN 0-8070-5430-5   [B]   MARC

Library of Congress   72

"LET YOUR MOTTO BE RESISTANCE"

"LET YOUR MOTTO BE RESISTANCE"

The Life and Thought of
Henry Highland Garnet

BY

EARL OFARI

BEACON PRESS   Boston

Copyright © 1972 by Earl Ofari
Library of Congress catalog card number: 72–75543
International Standard Book Number: 0–8070–5430–5
Beacon Press books are published under the auspices
of the Unitarian Universalist Association
Published simultaneously in Canada by Saunders of Toronto, Ltd.
Printed in the United States of America

Contents

REV. HENRY HIGHLAND GARNET,
PREACHING IN THE NATIONAL CAPITAL

An Acrostic

H ow noble and earnest, behold him stand
E loquent and faithful, in the Capital of the land
N ot Ciccro, or Chatham, with might sublime
R ehearsed such truths as this divine
Y ou feel his power—the pulscs thrill—

H e smites the oppressor with a will
I n cvcry soul of justice and love
G reat joy is found for above
L aurelled wreath or diadems
A nd jewelled crowns or sparkling gems
N or will thy glory ever depart
D crivcd from truth's immortal part

G od bless thee—standing like a rock
A noble hero in the battle's shock
R eceive the medal of honor due
N one more faithful of the "noble few"
E ndeavored to all, both far and near
T hy fame shall brighten from year to year

A.G.B.
Weekly Anglo-African, August 5, 1865

Introduction:
Toward a New Interpretation

The black liberation movement has deep historic roots in the American experience. From the rebellions on the slave ships to the recent rebellions in the cities, black people have been struggling against oppression. The pre–Civil War decades of the nineteenth century are of critical importance for an understanding of the recent character of this struggle. During that period black organizations were formed that would have an enormous impact on the entire thinking of the times. The tragedy is that only in the last few years has there been any concerted attempt to seriously analyze the period from a black perspective.

What had traditionally been presented as "Negro history" did not depart from the script of history as the great American success story. Negro history was nothing more than a pageant of the "exploits" and "accomplishments" of "noted" black figures. These individuals were usually considered "safe models" to hold before the public. Blacks from Douglass to Du Bois were systematically portrayed as Negroes who led fruitful and constructive lives in the best tradition of American society. This characterization stripped these blacks of their relevance to the black struggle. Their "deeds" were stressed while the forces that guided their thinking were ignored. That kind of history does not promote a grasp of the movements and issues of a given period. The mythologyzing of *individuals* does not lead to understanding. The creation of heroes should not be the aim of anyone truly concerned about liberation.

Blacks should look at a historical figure to learn methods and tactics used in the past that may have some value for their survival in the present. If the ideologies that shaped a person are not thoroughly examined, we generally end up knowing less at the finish than at the beginning of a study.

The proper study of black history will reveal movements that parallel those of today. Black nationalism in particular was as integral to thought in the middle of the nineteenth century as it is now.

We must begin to study the ideas of the blacks who have been consciously omitted from the historical record. Their approaches to the struggle must no longer be neglected. It makes absolutely no sense to have ten or fifteen biographies of Frederick Douglass and other black figures and not one definitive work on individuals such as Charles Langston, Frances Ellen Watkins, Sam R. Ward, Alexander Crummell, Robert Campbell, Bishop Holly, J. W. Loguen, Mammy Pleasant, the blacks who fought with John Brown, the slave rebels, and the national emigration conventions. No one would detract from the contributions of Douglass or anyone else; however, others have enriched the ideology of black struggle.

Rev. Henry Highland Garnet opened a new chapter in the black liberation movement when he said in 1843, "Let your motto be resistance." This was the real sentiment of the black masses. Like many others who have been overlooked, Garnet was an inspirational leader in the antislavery movement, but he also consistently took progressive stands on vital issues from free labor to anti-imperialism.

My aim in this study is to examine various facets of Garnet's life, from religion to black nationalism. An appendix with his major speeches and writings will enable the reader to follow the complete thrust of Garnet's thinking on important issues.

I wish to thank the staffs of the library of Cornell University, Syracuse University, the Rhodes House Library, the Schomburg Library, and the New York Historical Society for their gracious assistance in aiding my research. I must single out the following individuals for their valuable comments and criticisms: Ron Taylor, John Henrik Clarke, James Spady, Anne Kelley, Jeff Cooper, and Frank Greenwood. And, of course, special thanks must go to my wife, Yvonne, who provided key advice from start to finish.

"LET YOUR MOTTO BE RESISTANCE"

CHAPTER ONE

The Launching of a Career

In his *Capitalism & Slavery*, Eric Williams clearly notes that slavery was above all a highly organized institution for maximizing profit. At the height of its development, in the late seventeenth and early eighteenth centuries, chattel slavery existed as an intimate and self-serving feature of burgeoning industrial capitalism in the West:

> A racial twist has thereby been given to what is basically an economic phenomenon. Slavery was not born of racism: rather, racism was the consequence of slavery. Unfree labor in the New World was brown, white, black, and yellow; Catholic, Protestant and pagan.[1]

From 1800 on, the Southern planter class exercised an inordinate amount of control over the national government's operations. A fugitive slave act enacted in 1793 provided for the return of runaway slaves, by Northern state agencies—an indication of Southern power.

In the North the situation was little better for the tiny group of free blacks then residing in the major urban centers. Legislatures of Northern states had enacted laws designed to exclude blacks from voting, schools, public accommodations, and all but the most menial jobs.[2]

At the time of Henry Highland Garnet's birth on December 23, 1815, America had become an international bastion of slavery.

Born in New Market, Kent County, Maryland, Garnet's family, which included both parents and a sister, functioned as a unit even though in slavery. The cohesiveness of his family was an important factor in shaping Henry's early development. His grandfather had been a prince in the Mandingo empire in West Africa.* This too was important, for many traditions of West Africa were retained in the folklore and customs of plantation slaves, particularly those who had recently arrived in America.

When Garnet was nine, his family escaped from the New Market plantation of Colonel Spencer. The party of eleven was able to make its way to Bucks County, Pennsylvania. With the assistance of Thomas Garret, head of Pennsylvania's underground railroad, they continued safely to New York City, where George Garnet, Henry's father, resumed working as a shoemaker and soon became an important member of the African Methodist Episcopal Church. In 1826, Henry began to attend African Free School No. 1, founded in 1787 by the New York Manumission Society, most of whose members were wealthy financiers and politically prominent New Yorkers. The free school was an experiment to determine if young blacks could be instilled with white society's "better virtues" —thrift, industry, honesty—and proper manners. This completely fit in with the program of the manumission society, which sought the gradual abolition of slavery through legislative and moral action, the protection of free blacks from kidnaping and reenslavement, and the education of young blacks.[3]

* The Mandingo empire, which flourished in the thirteenth and fourteenth centuries, was a source of intellectual enlightenment for western Africa. The empire had large cities that were powerful commercial centers. At its height it "provided a striking example of the capacity of the Negro for political organization." See Basil Davidson, *The Lost Cities of Africa,* rev. ed. (Boston: Atlantic–Little, Brown, 1970), p. 98.

From the start, the city's black community had taken an active interest in the operation of the free school. Organizations such as the African Dorcas Association, a black female society, along with noted individuals such as Samuel Cornish and John Russwurm of *Freedom's Journal,* were especially active in the school's affairs. The established curricula concentrated on both the mechanical and the liberal arts. Whether intentionally or not, the school enabled some blacks to become self-sufficient through instruction in the trades.

Garnet excelled in all his studies at the school. He was conscious of oppression and desired to struggle against it. This was by no means unusual. The students at an early age developed a keen understanding of black oppression. One student in an address stated:

O Africa! the land of my fathers, ancestial of the sable exiles of America! My heart bleeds for thy children, while the clanking of their chains and the voice of their groaning ascend to the heaven like the blood of Abel.[4]

A great source of pride for Garnet and his schoolmates was the massive celebration by blacks of the abolition of slavery in New York. On July 5, 1827, nearly the entire black population of New York City turned out for a day of parades and speeches. Each of the city's black fraternal organizations was represented. They included the New York African Society for Mutual Relief, the Wilberforce Benevolent Society, and the Clarkson Benevolent Society. Hundreds of blacks from other states poured into New York for the celebration. Many of them were dressed in the colorful attire of the West Indies.

In 1829, Henry Garnet signed on board a schooner from New York City to Washington, D.C., as a cook and steward. Upon his return to New York, he learned that his family had been forced to scatter by slave catchers. His father, George, had saved himself only by an act of daring.

One of the slave catchers was a relative of Colonel Spencer, and as he approached the Garnet family's dwelling he made the mistake of calling out George's name. Immediately recognizing the voice, George Garnet told the catcher to wait while he checked to see if "George was at home." Mr. Garnet then walked quickly to the bedroom, jumped out the window, and escaped through a neighbor's back yard. Elizabeth Garnet, Henry's mother, found refuge with friends. In their absence from their home, their furniture was either stolen or destroyed by the slave catchers. Only Eliza, Henry's sister, was captured. She was tried as a "fugitive from labor" but was later released after convincing the recorder of the city that she had always been a resident of New York. Upon hearing that his family had fled, Henry Garnet purchased a large clasp knife and went searching throughout the city for their attackers. He gave up only after friends were able to convince him of the futility of his action.

The disruptions to his home and family life threw Henry completely on his own resources. As a consequence of the immediate threat to himself, he was sent by friends to live in Smithtown, Long Island, where for two years he worked on a farm as a contract laborer. While employed there, he lost the use of his right leg in an accident; later the leg had to be amputated.

In 1831, Henry decided to continue his education. When the opportunity arose, he enrolled in a New York City high school for colored youth set up by blacks to provide instruction in classical studies. This was an important step in Garnet's life. Many of the leaders that were to play a prominent role in the anti-slavery movement received fundamental instruction in schools organized by blacks for their own advancement. If blacks were to receive any kind of basic instruction, they had to provide it themselves. Before 1840, every Northern state had restricted the education black students could receive. Segregation was the norm in every school district.

These schools stimulated black students to search for

meaningful solutions to the problems that confronted the black community. Many students gained a perspective on politics, economics, world affairs, and, importantly, black history. Young black intellectuals were able to articulate the injustice that Northern blacks bitterly felt. Their attitudes were not simply the products of their education; they developed through struggle.

In 1835 Garnet was attending classes at Noyes Academy in Canaan, New Hampshire. The school, newly opened to blacks, was sponsored by the town's local anti-slavery society. The academy was regarded by progressive abolitionists in New Hampshire as an experiment to "prove" the capabilities of blacks for higher learning. Garnet, Alexander Crummell, and Thomas Sidney were the first black students to enroll at the academy. While there, Henry delivered his first formal speech before an abolitionist assembly. The occasion was the annual Independence Day meeting of the New Hampshire Anti-Slavery Society in nearby Plymouth, New Hampshire. Garnet, speaking after Crummell, called for the overthrow of slavery and rededication to the fight against oppression. He suggested that America should follow "the brilliant examples in the West Indies, South America, and the Cape of Good Hope," where slavery had recently been abolished.

Interestingly, both Crummell and Garnet denounced emigration to Liberia (Crummell would later defend it).[5]

This sentiment was in line with the stance of many white abolitionists, who publicly were opposed to the schemes of the colonizationists, although privately a number of them favored some plan for black repatriation. The American Colonization Society influenced the thinking of many anti-slavery sympathizers. The goal of the society, founded in 1816, was to establish a black colony in West Africa. The colony would be settled by free blacks from America.

Noyes Academy did not last long. A few weeks after the meeting, a group of farmers and townspeople from the surrounding area decided that the school should be closed. These whites were no longer willing to tolerate education for blacks. They wanted the fourteen black students in attendance at the academy removed not only from the school and the town but from the state. They dragged the school down with oxen and terrorized the students. Crummell, perhaps, best described Garnet's action at that instant:

> Under Garnet, as our leader, the boys in our boarding-house were moulding bullets, expecting an attack upon our dwelling. About eleven o'clock at night the tramp of horses was heard approaching, and as one rapid rider passed the house and fired at it, Garnet quickly replied by a discharge from a double-bar-relled shotgun which blazed away from the window. . . . That musket shot by Garnet doubtless saved our lives. The cowardly ruffians dared not attack us.[6]

After this incident, the black students were forced to leave New Hampshire. Garnet, Crummell, and Sidney traveled day and night under the worst conditions. They rode on top of carriages and on the deck of river boats because blacks were not allowed inside such passenger vehicles. To make matters even more difficult, Garnet was suffering from fever. In many of the villages and farm-houses they came to they often met with abuse.

The experience at Canaan had a profound effect on Garnet. He realized that in any struggle it is necessary to be able to back up agitation with physical threats. The roots of black oppression were deep within white American institutions. Thus appeals to ethics, morality, and truth would have only limited effects. When these appeals conflicted with entrenched economic and political interests, they became meaningless. Garnet realized that the ending of oppression required the exercise of a variety of tactics no matter how drastic. He prepared himself to meet the enemy on his own level. Garnet never again yielded on the question of freedom. Together with thirteen other black students, he vowed he would never celebrate the Fourth of July so long as slavery existed. The students formed a small society and resolved that when they had completed their education they would go to the South and foment slave rebellions.

In 1836, Garnet entered Presbyterian-affiliated Oneida Theological Institute to pursue his interest in religious and classical studies. Founded in 1826, Oneida, under the direction of Beriah Green when Garnet enrolled, was acknowledged by many as one of the most progressive institutions then in existence. Its approach to education was wholly innovative, organized around the manual labor concept newly introduced from Europe. Under this plan, the students worked and studied simultaneously.[7]

Oneida became popularly known for its role in championing the leading causes of the day. Marked as one of several model utopian communities, the institute attempted to instill in its students a spirit of cooperation and service to man. In 1834, the students there had founded what they believed to be the first anti-slavery society in New York state.* Two years later, Garnet attended as a delegate a meeting of the New York Anti-Slavery Society.

During the next few years at Oneida, Garnet involved himself in numerous causes. He and two other black students formed a committee in 1839 to protest the refusal of the Episcopal Church to admit Crummell to its General Theological Seminary in New York City. In a letter they condemned the action of the trustees:

We look upon the decision of the "Right Reverend Fathers in God," and those who concurred with it, with feelings of commingled grief, and horror. Inasmuch as they have presented no reasons for not

* The outspoken opposition of the institute to slavery coupled with the split in the Presbyterian Church led to its eventual demise. It was finally abandoned and sold to the Free Will Baptists in 1840.

receiving you into the "School of the Prophets," it is evident that it is nothing but the relation which you sustain to our oppressed brethren.[8]

After graduating from Oneida in September 1840, Garnet took up residence in Troy, New York, where he resided for the next eight years. He taught at the town's black school. Troy's black community had completed negotiations for the purchase of a Presbyterian church, and Garnet was immediately installed as a ruling elder. He worked to become a member of the Presbyterian clergy, studying under Rev. Amos Beman and Rev. Theodore Wright, two well-known black leaders. Garnet took special pleasure in studying under Wright, whom he had first met in 1833 while attending Sunday school classes at the First Colored Presbyterian Church in New York City. Garnet was finally licensed to preach by the Presbytery of Troy in 1842. In the same year he married Julia Williams. He had met her while attending school in New Hampshire. She had been a student at Prudence Crandall's boarding school, then the only high school for black girls. On many occasions Garnet praised her for her deep devotion to his work and to the freedom movement. He often credited her with being the source of many of the ideas he expressed in his speeches. In 1843, Garnet was ordained and appointed pastor of Troy's Liberty Street Presbyterian Church.

While immersed in his religious studies, Garnet had taken every opportunity to speak and write on questions that concerned the church. In a short article, "Shall Africa Have the Gospel," in the *Colored American* for July 24, 1841, he called for the employment of additional black missionaries and teachers in Africa. He viewed the continent "as a nation scattered and peeled" and asked, "Why is it that so few are found that are willing to help her?" To correct this neglect the Union Missionary Society was formed in 1841. Garnet, along with Beman, J. W. C. Pennington, and Wright, served on the executive committee. The society's goal was to involve more blacks in the African missionary movement.

During the period from the 1820's through the 1840's, blacks in New York began to protest their political disenfranchisement in the state. The New York Reform Convention in 1821 had voted age, residence, and property requirements for men seeking the ballot. Each man had to possess a freehold estate valued at $250. As intended, this measure kept an overwhelming majority of the state's black population from voting. Most of the estimated twenty thousand free blacks in New York were unskilled laborers, mechanics, servants, and sailors.[9] At a meeting in August 1837, in New York City with E. V. Clark as chairman and Garnet presiding as vice-president, a series of resolutions were drawn up in opposition to the property qualification. The meeting voted to circulate petitions, address appeals, and write a "General Address to the Colored Young Men Throughout the State." Another resolution urged the participants to pledge themselves "to each other, and to the colored young men of the state upon whom we call for a corresponding pledge." With this the meeting attempted to sound a note of black unity. On the motion of Garnet, it was resolved:

> That the laws which deprive free American citizens of the right to choose their rulers, are wholly unjust and anti-republican, and therefore ought to be immediately repealed.[10]

This meeting marked the start of the struggle against the property requirement for voting. The issue would provoke blacks for the next three decades.

Garnet's interest in the press began to grow. He saw it as a weapon that could be used to mold public opinion on the question of black rights. He became acquainted with Charles B. Ray, editor of the *Colored American* and well-known black abolitionist leader in New York. For a short time, Garnet served as a general agent for the paper in the state.

The *Colored American* was a pioneer in black journalism. Founded in 1837 as the *Weekly Advocate,* the paper grew under the skillful editorship of Samuel Cornish and later Ray. Its editors took uncompromising positions on abolition and black rights. They also provided many black writers with a vehicle for the expression of their ideas. The editors' aims were to directly secure the "moral, social, and political elevation and improvement of the free colored people; and the peaceful emancipation of the enslaved."[11]

As an agent, Garnet sought means to support the paper. At a local meeting of Albany blacks in June 1841, he praised the work of Ray and the *Colored American.* Two months later, at a black state convention in Troy, he proposed a "dollar plan." Each delegate was to contribute a dollar toward meeting the paper's expenses. This idea was incorporated into a resolution: "Resolved, That the *Colored American,* being identified with all our movements for political elevation, demands our support."[12]

Because of its inability to compete with the better-financed publications of the white abolitionists and the slow rise in black patronage, the *Colored American* gradually was pushed out of the market. The paper continued to champion the cause of black liberation until its final collapse in 1842. The importance of the paper as an organ in opposition to the Garrisonians should not be overlooked. William Z. Foster notes: "The *Colored American* . . . was anti-Garrison—with special stress upon the question of political action and the need for separate Negro organization."[13]

Inspired by the example of the *Colored American,* Garnet collaborated with William Allen, a black professor, and began publishing the *National Watchman* from Troy in 1842. Garnet tried to make the paper relevant to blacks.

Articles dealt mainly with occurrences in the anti-slavery movement. Often feature articles were about the special achievements of individual blacks. In one, Garnet wrote a short biographical sketch of James McCune Smith, emphasizing his educational attainments and his activities in the abolitionist movement. Smith was the first black doctor in the United States, having received his medical degree in 1837 from the University of Glasgow in Scotland.

The *National Watchman,* published in an area with a small black population, soon ran into the financial problems that had plagued the *Colored American.* Before its failure in 1847, Garnet had withdrawn from the editorship to publish his own newspaper, the *Clarion,* which lasted through only a few issues.

Garnet's venture into the newspaper business convinced him that blacks could manage and control their own press. Throughout the 1840's he spent considerable time trying to interest other blacks in the idea of an all-black press.

After 1830, the abolitionist movement began to gather steam. Societies were so numerous in New England that some abolitionists began to feel that a central body was needed to coordinate the movement's activities. This led to the formation of the American Anti-Slavery Society in 1833. The goal of the society, led by William Lloyd Garrison and his supporters, was the "intellectual, moral and religious improvement" of blacks.[14]

The society's members tended to view the struggle as a moral battle against the "evils of slavery." They considered blacks to be limited in character in comparison to whites, and they thought blacks should be brought "up" to white standards. Despite the paternalism that tainted the thinking of the society's members, many blacks readily lent their support to the new group. Northern blacks seemed willing to aid any organization demonstrating an intention to fight for the improvement of their condition. Thus seven blacks were at the founding convention of the society; of this group, three, James McCrummell, James Barbadoes, and Robert Purvis, signed the organization's Declaration of Sentiments.

Garnet's activities as a writer and speaker increasingly drew the attention of those prominent in the established abolitionist societies. Garnet displayed a flair for the dramatic in his addresses. He was a master of the use of wry wit and sarcasm to emphasize many of his points. Once during the middle of a speech a listener who did not like Garnet's remarks threw a pumpkin at him. Garnet ducked. The pumpkin splattered over the stage. Without breaking stride, he quietly said, "My good friends, do not be alarmed, it is only a soft pumpkin; some gentleman has thrown away his head, and lo! his brains are dashed out!" On another occasion, when asked by a race-baiting white whether Garnet would advise him to marry a "dirty, stinking, greasy, black, negro wench," Garnet snapped back, "But would you have me marry a dirty, stinking, greasy white wench?"* Garnet had to be tough on the lecture circuit. In the early years abolitionist speakers had to be prepared for anything. They often experienced physical assault, and verbal abuse was common. In some cases Garnet's life literally depended on the skill he used to defuse a potentially dangerous situation. Garnet proved himself more than equal to the task.

In May 1840, he was invited to deliver a lecture at the seventh anniversary meeting of the American Anti-Slavery Society. He opened his speech† with the following resolution:

That all the rights and immunities of American citizens are justly due to the people of color, who have ever been, and still are, willing to contribute their

* Quoted from James McCune Smith, *Sketch of the Life and Labors of Rev. Henry Highland Garnet* (Washington: 1865), pp. 31–32.
† The complete text of this speech is in Appendix One.

full share to enrich and to defend our common country.[15]

He stressed the need to examine the deeds of the many blacks who shed their blood to gain the liberties that white Americans enjoyed. It was blacks, Garnet contended, who were the real heroes of the American Revolution:

> It is with pride that I remember, that in the earliest attempts to establish democracy in this hemisphere, colored men stood by the side of your fathers, and shared with them the toils of the revolution. . . . No monumental piles distinguish their "dreamless beds." Scarcely an inch on the page of history has been appropriated to their memory. Yet truth will give them a share of the fame that was reaped upon the field of Lexington and Bunker Hill.

He pointed out that the unrequited labor of blacks had developed not only the industry of the South but America as a whole. Taking a stab at American churches for their inaction on black oppression, Garnet bitterly said:

> Church and state, the one holding up a Christianity, falsely so called, immersed in blood and the other endeavoring to shield itself behind law, have united in platting a scourge, with which they have whipped him away from the highest privileges, and driven him into the most hopeless darkness.

In the same month, Garnet attended the founding convention of the American and Foreign Anti-Slavery Society. The society was formed by New York abolitionists led by Gerrit Smith, William Goodell, and Arthur and Lewis Tappan, in opposition to the policies of the Garrison-controlled American Anti-Slavery Society. The New Yorkers favored direct political action to combat slavery; the Garrisonians held to the position of moral suasion.

After 1840, Garnet began to concentrate his energy on specific needs and problems of the black community. One of them was the continuing struggle for black suffrage in New York.

CHAPTER TWO

The Developing Struggle

During the summer of 1840, the *Colored American* called
for a convention to be held in Albany in August. The purpose of the convention was for blacks to discuss measures
to be used to gain political power. On the surface, there
seemed to be nothing unusual about such a convention.
In the past decade regional and state conventions had been
held by blacks. The Albany convention, however, was to
be different. The sponsors made it clear that for the first
time a convention was to be run exclusively by blacks.

Garnet, his cousin Sam R. Ward, Crummell, Ray, and
Theodore Wright were the main backers of this policy.
They felt that blacks must begin to take the initiative in
planning and implementing programs to alleviate their
situation. Whites would not be excluded, but their participation would be kept to a minimum. Such a move was
necessary because whites were not always serious about
the struggle for black rights.

The sponsors perceived the ambivalence white abolitionists felt about tactics. Many appeared willing to carry the
struggle only to a limited point. They emphasized moral
appeals and almost completely ignored the political and
economic oppression of blacks.

Garnet and the others felt that the white anti-slavery
movement was riddled with racism. Often when black
leaders addressed abolitionist gatherings they would men-

tion this problem. Wright, at the annual meeting of the American Anti-Slavery Society in 1837, remarked:

> It is an easy thing to ask about the vileness of the slavery at the South, but to call the dark man a brother, heartily to embrace the doctrine advanced in the second article of the constitution, to treat all men according to their moral worth, to treat the man of color in all circumstances as a man and brother—that is the test. . . . Abolitionists must annihilate in their own bosoms the chord of caste.[1]

Some anti-slavery groups did not even admit blacks. Others, though not officially excluding them, did not go out of their way to welcome them as members. In Pennsylvania, a leading abolitionist organization, the Society for Promoting the Abolition of Slavery, from 1775 to 1859 admitted only one black, Robert Purvis. Although blacks were part of the American Anti-Slavery Society, much was left to be desired. At meetings of the society's executive committee, members heatedly debated the question of social intercourse with blacks, which many opposed. The organization never addressed any of its literature to the slaves themselves. Article 3 of the society's constitution forbade its members to "countenance the oppressed in vindicating their rights by resorting to physical force." Jane and William Pease make the following observation about the society:

> Toward Negroes, in short, the Society's attitude was clearly paternalistic. . . . Each agent was advised to locate some white person in every community he visited, a "tried friend of the colored people," to keep an eye out for them and to act as "friend, adviser, and protector;" it might be added *in loco parentis*.[2]

Some of the tracts distributed by white abolitionists depicted blacks as individuals with capabilities equal to those of whites. However, white abolitionists were nearly united in the opinion that blacks were intellectually inferior to whites. This precipitated the view that blacks were little more than children in need of guidance. According to George M. Frederickson, "by the early 1840's the anti-slavery movement itself provided fertile soil for romantic racialism, a doctrine which acknowledged permanent racial differences but rejected the notion of a clearly defined racial hierarchy."[3]

The convention's sponsors were not surprised when white abolitionists attacked them. The first assault was an editorial in the *National Anti-Slavery Standard,* a widely read abolitionist weekly:

> We are not opposed to the holding of a Convention for the purpose of seeing what can be done to remove the disabilities of our friends the country over; but we do oppose a Convention of colored citizens. We oppose all exclusive action on the part of the colored people.[4]

The *Colored American* immediately responded to this. One of its editors, known simply as "A," wrote:

> We have shown what we consider a necessary cause for exclusive action; we will now endeavor to prove that no people ever succeeded in establishing their principles, or regaining their rights without "exclusive action" on their part, where they had the power so to act.[5]

In a letter to the *Standard,* Ward put the matter in clearer perspective:

> The continuation of wrongs, injustice, and ingratitude, inflicted upon us by the State government, the small share of sympathy evinced towards us by many of our professed friends, and the still smaller amount of efficient action put forth by them in our behalf, all

render it indispensably necessary that the colored people of this State should convene and act for themselves.[6]

Other white abolitionists chose simply to ignore the Albany convention. A group of them threw their support to the American Moral Reform Society's convention scheduled for later in the summer at New Haven, Connecticut. Those attending this convention, under the sponsorship of David Ruggles and William Whipper, adhered to the principle of interracial action.

The Albany convention got under way on the appointed date. Forty delegates attended its opening session. Charles B. Ray was elected chairman; Garnet, C. L. Reason, and William Topp were chosen secretaries. During the three-day gathering a number of resolutions were offered. The business committee put forth one calling upon blacks "throughout the state to become possessors of the soil." Garnet and several other delegates opposed this resolution. They felt that owning land did not guarantee that the rights of blacks would be respected. To them, landownership was not a viable solution to the problem of disenfranchisement. They believed that the property provision in the law was devised by the state to suppress blacks. If they acquired property and fulfilled that qualification, the state would probably erect another barrier to prevent them from voting. A frontal attack on the entire act was required. A measure detrimental to the interests of the black community should be fought, not conformed to.

Despite opposition, the convention passed a modified resolution urging blacks in New York to purchase land "because it guarantees permanency of residence."[7] The delegates appointed a committee to compile statistics on the number and condition of the state's black schools, churches, and other institutions. They decided to initiate a petition campaign to the state legislature, requesting repeal of the suffrage restrictions. The idea of the petitions was announced in an address that the convention drafted to the people of New York. Garnet was largely responsible for the actual writing of it.

The address was a moderate appeal to the powers of the state to reconsider their policy toward blacks. It emphasized that blacks were citizens and should be permitted to exercise all the rights of citizens. Specifically, this meant political participation. The address repeated a familiar theme:

> We do regard the right of our birthdom, our service in behalf of the country, contributing to its importance, and developing its resources, as favorable considerations —considerations adapted to banish all thought of proscription and injustice, from the power holding body of the country, and to lead them to a hearty and practical acknowledgement of the claims and rights of a disfranchised people.[8]

In the address were demands for adherence to the principles set down in the Declaration of Independence and the Constitution. If black people had to pay taxes and obey the law, then, at the least, they should enjoy equal rights and protection under that law:

> And we say it is injustice of the most aggrieved character, either to deprive us of a just and legitimate participation in the rights of the state, or to make us bear the burdens, and submit to its enactments, when all its arrangements, plans, and purposes, are framed and put into operation utterly regardless of us.[9]

Although the address and the mood of the convention were conciliatory, they did indicate the blacks' willingness to unite over issues of immediate concern to their community. Further, the convention stimulated interest among the state's blacks in the question of political rights.

In the following months, the petition drive was carried on throughout New York. The plan was to have an elected delegation deliver the petitions directly to the state legislature at its opening session in mid-February 1841. As chairman of the central committee, Garnet was given the responsibility of coordinating the campaign.

In an article in the *Colored American,* he announced that the convention was seeking six thousand signatures from New York City alone. He chastised blacks who failed to get enough signatures on their petitions and reminded the petition's sponsors:

> The legislature is now in session. He that would prosper, must arise early, and begin his labor with a willing heart and a vigorous arm. Heretofore, it has been a fault with us that we have sent in our petitions at too late an hour; and thus amid the hurry that generally attends the close of the session, they have been neglected or laid aside. Then, brethren, in consideration of this fact will you awake and bestir yourselves immediately?[10]

Garnet and the convention members were prepared to use the petition as the main weapon to mobilize black sentiment. They felt that with enough push a sufficient number of signatures could be secured to force the legislature to act on their demands. During the following weeks, Garnet doubled his efforts to reach the black community with petitions. By February 2, he was able to report that thirteen hundred signatures had been received from New York City. The petitions were presented to the legislature at its opening session in February 1841. Garnet used the occasion to address the body on the franchise question and its relationship to New York blacks. However, the legislature took no action.

It was then decided to hold another convention to discuss further strategy. Garnet immediately issued the convention call. He and the six members who comprised the central committee thought the petitions should be resubmitted to the state legislature at its next yearly session. The

convention's goal, stated in the call, was to lay the ground-
work for "greeting the ears of our legislators at their next
session [with] our petitions."[11]

The convention was scheduled for August 1841 in Troy.
Most of those who had attended the first convention were
present. The delegates again announced their intention to
present the petitions to the state legislature.

When the petitions were submitted the second time, the
legislature again took no action. The sponsors were disappointed but still determined to carry on the fight.

Another state convention was held in Rochester in August 1843. Garnet again was appointed chairman of the
central committee and was assigned the task of present-
ing to the governor the convention's request that "he make
favorable mention of the extension of the franchise to the
people of color in his annual message." A follow-up suffrage convention was held in Syracuse in August 1845;
Ray was president and Garnet was head of the business
committee. From this position, Garnet offered a resolution
that stated "that adopted citizens having escaped the oppression of their own countries, ought to remember us
when it goes well with them."[12] This apparently was a
reference to the large numbers of recent immigrants from
Europe, particularly Irish and Germans, who tended to join
right in in the oppression of blacks. In his address to the
Syracuse convention, Garnet implored blacks "to never
give up the ship," saying that the only way they could
accomplish their tasks was through "united, vigorous
action."[13]

This did not mark the end of the suffrage campaign.
Blacks continued to meet to discuss methods for obtaining
the vote. Garnet did not relent on the issue. He began to
encourage blacks to invest in land outside of the city. In a
report* drafted at a convention held in Schenectady in
1844, he called upon blacks to gain land in order "to rise
above independence":

* The complete text of this report is in Appendix Two.

Let our men become the owners of the soil, and they shall be the founders of towns and villages; and as they grow up, they may grow with them, and may give tone and character to a just and liberal public sentiment.[14]

This represented a shift in Garnet's position. He had begun to feel that perhaps land could serve as an instrument for securing both political and economic power.

Even though those active in the suffrage campaign did not entirely achieve their goal, the movement was not a failure. Despite blockage of proposals for equal political rights, by 1851 the estimated five thousand black voters in New York had formed a bloc that the major political parties could not ignore.

On the basis of his involvement with the conventions, Garnet concluded that it was time for blacks to take decisive political action to obtain their rights. Weighing the situation, he felt that they must align themselves with a party that had a program for their advancement. The newly organized Liberty Party seemed to offer such a program.

Formed in 1840, the Liberty Party constructed no barriers to black involvement in politics. It proclaimed itself a party dedicated to the overthrow of slavery. Garnet, quickly satisfied, joined the party. Along with J. W. Loguen, a black minister, and Ward, Garnet lectured throughout New York on behalf of the party. Although it received few votes and little recognition in its first three years of existence, the Liberty Party did manage to convince some blacks that it had a future and thereby deserved their support.

In February 1842, Garnet attended the party's convention in Massachusetts as a delegate from New York. He delivered one of the session's principal addresses.* He be-

---

* The complete text of this speech is in Appendix Three.

gan by noting that slavery had affected every individual in America. To end slavery, it was necessary to "feel for the slaves 'as bound with them,' we must place ourselves, so far as we can, in their position, and go forward with the fixed consciousness that we are *free* or *enslaved* with them."[15] In this speech, Garnet hinted that those sincerely concerned with freedom and justice should welcome slave rebellions:

> Ah, sir, those heaving fires that formerly burst forth like the lava of a burning volcano, upon the inhabitants of Southampton and elsewhere, when the colored man rose and asserted *his rights to humanity and liberty,* are kept in chock, only by the abolitionists. They hold open the safety valve of the nation;— and these *enemies of the country,* as they are called, are the very men, sir, that prevent a general insurrection of the slaves from spreading carnage and devastation throughout the entire South.[16]

Garnet viewed the Liberty Party as a constructive agent within the anti-slavery movement. He totally committed himself to defend its principles. He expressed this feeling in a resolution labeling those who opposed the party as being uninformed about its objects.

During the next year, the party attracted a large number of abolitionist supporters to its ranks. To consolidate its gains, the party's backers scheduled a convention for Buffalo in August 1843. This convention was an important step for blacks' political participation. According to Charles H. Wesley:

> The Buffalo Convention of the Liberty Party was the most significant convention in the history of the Negro's political life in the United States prior to the Civil War. . . . This was the first time in American history that Negro citizens were actually in the leadership of a political convention.[17]

Delegates gathered at the convention from all over the New England area. Many of those who came were prominent figures in established abolitionist societies. Among the black delegates were Garnet, Ray, and Ward. Garnet was appointed to the committee of nominations, and Ray was placed on the roll committee.

In his address to the convention, Garnet offered the following resolution:

Resolved, That the Liberty Party has not been organized for any temporary purpose by interested politicians, but has arisen from among the people, in consequence of a conviction, hourly gaining ground, that no other Party in the country represents the true principles of American Liberty or the true spirit of the Constitution of the United States.[18]

The convention passed forty-four resolutions. Most condemned the government for its role in perpetuating slavery. The resolutions called for direct political action by dedicated anti-slavery foes and legislative action to nullify the sections of the Constitution that could be construed to be supportive of slavery. The party went on record in favor of popular measures such as increased education, control of local government, redistribution of land, and free labor. After some debate, the party stated its opposition to the federal government's use of the army and the militia to suppress slave rebellions: "When freemen unsheath the sword it should be to strike for liberty, not for despotism."

After the convention, the party formally engaged Garnet to lecture among blacks throughout New York on the party's aims and goals. From October to December 1843, he combed the state, speaking to groups and urging their support for the party's program. Garnet's staunch advocacy of the party's principles soon led him into a clash with other black abolitionist leaders.

At a national Negro convention held in Buffalo two weeks prior to the convention of the Liberty Party, Garnet had attempted to introduce several resolutions that would have placed the convention on record in support of the party. In the debate that followed, the resolutions were vigorously opposed by Frederick Douglass, Charles Lenox Remond, and a few others who were closely associated with the Garrisonians. At the time, in fact, both Douglass and Remond were paid lecturers for the Massachusetts Anti-Slavery Society, an offshoot of the larger American Anti-Slavery Society. These blacks, in line with Garrison, could not see committing the convention to a policy of direct political involvement. Although Garnet's resolutions were subsequently adopted, the opposition was not prepared to accept the majority decision. In a letter to the *National Anti-Slavery Standard* on October 5, 1845, William Wells Brown (who would later achieve fame as a black novelist and playwright), a member of the faction opposing Garnet, wrote:

> Mr. Garnet knew, as did every member of that convention, that there were more than two that voted against the resolution adopting the views of the liberty party; yet Mr. Garnet singled out Remond and Douglass as the only ones that voted against the resolution. Why did he single them out? If he wished to single out two, why did he not single out some other two?

Brown clearly saw in Garnet's attack on Douglass and Remond an attack on the Garrison-backed societies. For this, both Garnet and the Liberty Party had to be thoroughly repudiated. Douglass, later recounting his differences with the party, put it simply: "We were opposed to carrying the anti-slavery cause to the ballot-box, and they believed in carrying it there. They looked at slavery as a creature of law; we regarded it as a creature of public opinion."[19]

This was not the end of the controversy. Newspapers in harmony with the Garrisonians often attacked Garnet. An article in the *National Anti-Slavery Standard*, on September 8, 1843, flatly charged him with seeking to exploit the problems in the black community in order to make converts to the Liberty Party. It also asserted that he had used a public meeting on the issue of black suffrage to push the party's program. The reporter observed:

> It was nearly midnight when I left. Mr. Garnet was then speaking not on the merits of the question, but was making a Liberty Party harangue, and endeavoring to show it to be the duty of all colored men to vote with that party.

Undaunted, Garnet continued to uphold the party line when addressing black audiences. He was willing to do this because he saw the Liberty Party as a positive force for change. It was the only political grouping on the scene to hold out any promise for securing black rights. In his view, the other parties existed merely to do the bidding of reactionary Northern merchants and the Southern planters. Garnet's belief that moral appeals should have no place in the anti-slavery fight found ready acceptance among party adherents. He hoped the black movement as a whole would come to support this position.

Throughout the remainder of the Liberty Party's brief existence Garnet remained a faithful follower. Even when the party was on the verge of dissolution in 1848, Garnet attended its convention and delivered an address.

A campaign had been growing to end segregation in public transportation. In most Northern cities, laws required blacks to sit in separate compartments on coaches. Many abolitionists joined in community efforts to legalize equal travel accommodations. In 1842 Remond delivered a report before the Massachusetts House of Representatives denouncing segregated transportation.

It was fairly common for blacks to be assaulted on public carriages in Northern cities. In the summer of 1848 Garnet himself was beaten and dragged from a railroad car in Buffalo when he refused to give up his seat in the "white section." He was on his way to Canada at the time to address a temperance meeting. The editor of a Buffalo newspaper, the *Daily Propeller,* demanded that all sympathetic persons in the city come forth and express their indignation over the incident. As a gesture of support, the paper published a letter from Garnet describing the circumstances of the attack. Garnet proclaimed his right to defend himself. He noted that the incident had not happened in the South. The blame had to be laid on Northern racism:

> While I would not wish to injure those who have injured me, I would at the same time beg the public to decide whether it is just, humane, or necessary, thus to treat an American citizen, who is guilty of no crime. In justice to the people of the South, whom the Northern dough-faces make the scape goats of their villainy and outrage, I would say that there is no evidence that they demand any such gratuitous servility and inhumanity.[20]

The entire abolitionist press joined in condemning the attack. Douglass' *North Star* carried successive articles on the incident. Garnet had been active for some time in the struggle against segregated travel. As recently as two months before the attack, he had toured New York and Rhode Island, where at public meetings he condemned the railroads for their racist practices.

During this period, Garnet began to devote some of his energy to the temperance movement. In the 1830's a number of temperance societies had been organized within the Northern black communities. Often they were run in association with the larger white societies. Their goal was the elimination of alcohol consumption among blacks. Temperance advocates considered alcohol to be one of the chief causes for idleness, crime, family neglect, and other undesirable behavior. These traits, they believed, contributed to whites' adverse stereotypes of blacks.

After 1835, the temperance cause began to assume greater importance for the abolitionist movement. Black abolitionists supported temperance out of practical necessity. To wage a serious struggle for liberation, it was essential that blacks be conscious and aware at all times of the situations they faced. They had to be sober to plan strategies and tactics to meet the problems that continually faced the black community. Temperance thus became solidly linked with the freedom struggle.

Garnet in his lectures often connected temperance and the struggle for black rights. He was a member of several temperance societies. In July 1846 he delivered the main address at a meeting of the Delevan Temperance Union held at Poughkeepsie, New York. Garnet told the audience that black self-improvement depended on clear and alert thought:

Men and women, descendants of Africa: our ancestors were distinguished for their wisdom in the arts and sciences. If you would imitate their good example —if you would find the lost pearl which they treasured up for their children, you must be strangers to the intoxicating cup; for intemperance stupefies the mind and mars its beauty.[21]

At a Daughters of Temperance meeting held in Philadelphia in November 1848, Garnet repeated this idea. Upon finishing his two-hour lecture, he was hailed by the gathering as "the apostle of liberty and temperance."

The movement to acquire land, which had been given expression in 1840 at the Albany convention, began to gain momentum among blacks. Many saw landownership as a way to build self-sufficiency within the group. According to the proponents of land settlement, progress could be made only when blacks were able to provide for their own needs. To a certain extent, this made sense. In the 1840's, land in America was cheap and plentiful. Despite restrictions in some areas against blacks' owning land, groups of blacks could acquire and work it on a cooperative basis. This led to the success of the famed Buxton settlement in Canada, which stood as a model of black economic independence.

New York blacks had to consider the property qualification of the state's suffrage law. Some still believed that the surest way to obtain the franchise was to get some land. Many white abolitionists encouraged blacks to acquire land. They thought that owning property would develop stability and industriousness among the black people and would help integrate them into the general social order.

In 1846, Gerrit Smith, a wealthy New York abolitionist landholder, proposed to divide more than one hundred twenty thousand acres of his land in upstate New York into small farms for black occupancy. According to Smith's plan, the land would be distributed among blacks who showed a disposition to develop it. To carry out his plan, Smith needed agents. One of the first persons he approached was Garnet, with whom he had been acquainted for several years. Garnet had so admired Smith's work in the anti-slavery movement that he had considered at one time moving to western New York, where Smith resided, to coordinate his activities with Smith's. Eventually, 1,985 grants were made under Garnet's supervision. Among those who received titles to land were Douglass, Remond, and William C. Nell.

Smith viewed land distribution primarily as a method of increasing the number of black voters in the state. He never looked on it as a way of breaking up the large estates owned by the wealthy power magnates. Land distribution was not aimed at fundamentally reorganizing the mechanisms of control.

In contrast, the blacks who assisted Smith had a different view. Garnet saw land distribution as a means not only of increasing blacks' political power but also of promoting genuine democratic control of the governing processes. Unlike Smith, Garnet was not concerned with making a few blacks respectable and well-off. Nor was he especially concerned about fitting blacks into the status quo. In analyzing the political system. Garnet concluded that power in America was held by a white monied and propertied class. This was particularly true in the South, where about three hundred thousand slaveholders out of a population of eight million whites exercised total control over the government. Garnet noted:

> The chains of the last slave on earth may be broken in twain, and still, while the unholy system of land-lordism prevails, nations and people will mourn. But the moment that this wide-spread and monstrous evil is destroyed, the dawn of the gospel day will break forth, and the world will have rest.[22]

He foresaw that simply ending slavery would neither break the power of the rich controllers nor ensure any meaningful program for black liberation.* It was necessary to totally destroy the class that held power if blacks *and* whites were ever to progress:

> Again: let slavery be abolished in this country, and let the land and the labor monopolists have three or four hundred years the start of the emancipated, and still the free men will be heavy laden, with an uphill course before them. Herein lies the secret of the trouble in the British West Indies. The old slave-holders are the landlords, and such they intend to be.[23]

* A few black activists had for years been conscious of the relation between organized wealth and the political establishment. The *Weekly Advocate*, a black newspaper founded in 1837 by Philip A. Bell, stated in its first editorial: "We shall advocate Universal Suffrage and Universal Education, and we shall oppose all Monopolies, which oppress the Poor and laboring classes of society."

Garnet was not the only black leader expressing such ideas. Douglass, who also worked closely with Smith on his land program, took a similar position. Describing himself as a Chartist, he wrote: "What justice is there in the general Government giving away, as it does, the millions upon millions of acres of public lands, to aid soulless railroad corporations to get rich?"[24]

The views of black abolitionists such as Garnet and Douglass on the question of land and power clearly marked them as pacesetters of the freedom movement. They anticipated some of the ideals that populist as well as socialist groups would incorporate in their programs. Garnet knew that radical measures were needed to help impoverished blacks in the North. To call for anything less would betray his responsibility as a leader.

Garnet became involved in nearly every phase of the land movement. He wanted to make sure that families who agreed to occupy land had a fair chance to succeed in developing it. Resettlement was especially difficult for blacks who had lived in the city. It required a great deal of personal sacrifice. In consideration of this, Garnet persistently reminded blacks of the importance of their tasks. In a special sermon delivered to a group of black settlers departing for their new land, he elaborated:

> I believe that it is God's design that every man shall have a home. This grand design will be consummated as fast as men become enlightened and just. The complete reign of gospel principles, will introduce a perfect system of agrarianism. . . . There is something solemn, and important in the settlement of every new country. It is like entering into a new world. The first settlers of a country are to a great extent, the index to the history of succeeding generations.[25]

Aware of the grantees' importance as future voters (they would be able to meet the property qualification) and, more significantly, as possible Liberty Party supporters, Garnet exhorted:

> Be interested in the political affairs of the nation, and see to it that your first and last votes are given in the fear of God, and for men who do not oppress, and enslave their fellow men. Refuse to vote for those who will give honor to oppressors.[26]

The events of the early 1840's had a profound effect on the consciousness of Garnet and other black leaders. These men and women, no longer bound to the strictures of the past, were willing to experiment with new concepts and devise new tactics to combat oppression. Up until this time, it had been an almost unchallenged belief among abolitionists that the struggle against slavery was one of right and truth against evil. The programs of the anti-slavery societies were always formulated within the framework of moral suasion. Any deviation from this, as Garnet found, was frowned on within established abolitionist circles.

As conditions of Northern blacks continued to deteriorate and as the power of the planters grew, it was inevitable that young black abolitionists would reject nonviolence. Impetus was given to this thinking by the new movement toward separate organizations for blacks and whites. Above all, though, the greatest single force to give currency to a militant mood was the activities of the slaves themselves.

CHAPTER THREE

Prophet of Revolutionary Black Nationalism

Violence began with a vision of "white spirits and black spirits engaged in battle . . . in the heavens."[1] When it ended, sixty whites lay dead in Southampton, Virginia. The rebellion in 1831, the greatest of the time, was led by a slave preacher named Nat Turner. It sent shock waves throughout the nation.

The Turner uprising was the best known of many slave revolts. By 1830, nearly every locale in the South had experienced some form of disturbance from the slave population. In the swamp areas of eastern Virginia, the Carolinas, and Florida, small groups of maroons (runaway slaves) lived at various times.

The activities of the slaves provided the abolitionist movement with an interesting dilemma. Should abolitionists continue to view slavery only in terms of right and virtue, or should they begin to assist slave rebels? Garrison and his supporters, though deploring the conditions of slavery, opposed the type of actions taken by Turner. To their credit, however, a few courageous whites did buck the tide, supporting and even participating in slave revolts. These precursors to John Brown included Ruel Blake, A. L. Donovan, John Fairfield, and George Boxley.

Garnet had not yet taken a firm position on the question

of slave revolts. In his speech at the Liberty Party convention in 1842 he indicated guarded approval of slave violence but did not depart from the general attitudes of other abolitionists. By early 1843, though, his opinion had begun to change. Garnet slowly came to believe that not only did slaves have the right to rebel, but that abolitionists had the right to support them. The slaves, he thought, could through their actions weaken the system from within and eventually destroy it. In any case, win or lose, the slaves had to assume responsibility for their liberation and not depend on aid from abolitionists, which was not likely to be soon forthcoming. The oppressed would have to fight, kill, and die for liberation.

A national Negro convention had been scheduled in Buffalo for the end of August 1843. It was to be the first such gathering since the Negro conventions of the early 1830's and was considered the most important black meeting of the year. An unusual amount of planning had gone into the convention. In May in New York City a preliminary meeting with Theodore Wright as chairman and A. J. Gordon as secretary was held to discuss proposed guidelines that the convention would follow. Delegates attended the meeting from Massachusetts, Connecticut, New York, New Jersey, Pennsylvania, and Ohio. The sponsoring committee at the meeting declared that it was the duty of the oppressed to conduct their own struggle, organization was a necessity, and blacks should begin holding Negro conventions with regularity because they were a plausible means for effecting black unity. Garnet, who was present, joined with fifty other persons in signing this proclamation.

On the appointed date in August, more than seventy delegates gathered in Buffalo to begin the convention proceedings. Garnet was elected chairman of the committee of correspondence. He opened the convention by reading the call. Upon his motion, Samuel Davis was installed as temporary convention chairman. Davis proceeded to deliver an address that set the tone for the convention. He called upon blacks to dispense with petitions and begin a campaign of direct action to secure their rights. He urged blacks as a group to develop their own resources and lead their own organizations:

> If we sit down in idleness and sloth waiting for them [the whites] or any other class of men to do our own work, I fear it will never be done. If we are not willing to rise up and assert our own cause we have no reason to look for success. We, ourselves, must be willing to contend for the rich boon of our freedom and equal rights, or we will never enjoy the boon.[2]

In addition to his duties on the correspondence committee, Garnet was appointed to the nine-man business committee as chairman. The convention had invested this committee with much of the power to determine the issues and proposals to be discussed. Given this mandate, Garnet offered a resolution endorsing the Liberty Party. The committee's other resolutions included promotion of agricultural pursuits, the acquisition of land, and the creation of a national press controlled by blacks. To effect this last proposal, the committee recommended that the convention establish a seven-member committee to organize a paper, obtain the services of an editor and publisher, and direct its management.

As the convention progressed, many observers thought that the black delegates were infected with a spirit of independence, which had often been lacking at similar gatherings. The speakers' denunciations of injustice and their appeals for blacks to unite seemed more forceful. The new feeling soon received dramatic expression when Garnet took the podium. The speech he was to deliver had been formally prepared and entitled "An Address to the Slaves of the United States of America."*

* The complete text of this speech is in Appendix Four.

In his opening sentence Garnet clearly stated that his words were meant for the slaves exclusively and that he intended to break with past practices:

> Your brethren of the North, East, and West have been accustomed to meet together in National Conventions, to sympathize with each other, and to weep over your unhappy condition. In these meetings we have addressed all classes of the free, but we have never, until this time, sent a word of consolation and advice to you.

This was a sharp rebuke to previous conventions, dominated by whites, which always had been careful not to formulate resolutions or permit speeches that could be interpreted as a call to the slaves to take action. Garnet briefly reviewed the facts of slavery. He urged blacks to take the lead in the fight against it: "You can plead your own cause, and do the work of emancipation better than any others."

In the key section of his speech, Garnet said:

> You had far better all die—*die immediately,* than live slaves, and entail your wretchedness upon your posterity. If you would be free in this generation, here is your only hope. However much you and all of us may desire it, there is not much hope of redemption without the shedding of blood. If you must bleed, let it all come at once—rather *die freemen, than live to be the slaves.*

He continued by praising the uprisings of Vessey, Turner, Joseph Cinque, Madison Washington, and other slave rebels. After blasting the government for attempting to spread slavery to Canada and Mexico, he ended on a note of black unity, reminding the slaves that there is strength in numbers and that "you are three millions."

Without doubt, the speech had the desired impact. One reporter observed:

> So powerful was the denunciation, that one of the first clergymen of the city, an anti-abolitionist, was heard on going out, to declare, that were he to act from the impulse of the moment, he should shoulder his musket and march South.
>
> Here, Editor, was true eloquence—the ridiculous, the pathetic, the indignant, all called into irresistible action; and I cannot but think, that had it been one of our white orators, instead of Garnet, he would have been lauded to the skies.[3]

As expected, the address was the subject of much debate by convention participants. Before the move was made for adoption, the speech was referred to the business committee. Ray, a committee member, thought it should be presented to a committee of five, which he hoped Garnet would be selected to chair. Basically in agreement with Garnet, Ray wanted the address to

> pass through a close and critical examination and perceiving some points in it that might in print appear objectionable, to have it somewhat modified, and also that it might proceed forth from a special committee of which the author should be the chairman and thus receive the usual credit due to chairmen of committees presenting documents to public bodies.[4]

After further discussion, the speech was presented to the convention, where it was defeated by one vote.[5] Apparently the immediate reason for the speech's failure to be adopted was the abstention from voting of several of its supporters. Ray himself declined to vote because, he explained, he had been too busy with committee work to follow the debate on the matter. At the end of the convention, he announced that he was in favor of the speech and would have voted for its adoption. A subsequent effort was made by the speech's backers to present it to the convention for another vote. This failed when it was decided to adjourn the convention at the scheduled time.

Following a familiar pattern, the main opposition to Garnet's speech came from the Garrisonians: Douglass, Brown, and Remond. Douglass, listing the reasons for his opposition, suggested that there was "too much physical force in both the address and the speaker." He felt that such an address, if adopted, might spark a mass insurrection, which would accomplish nothing. Writing later, Garnet summarized the objections to the speech:

> (1) That the document was war-like, and encouraged insurrection; and (2) That if the convention should adopt it, that those delegates who lived near the borders of the slave states, would not dare to return to their homes.[6]

These were more than just academic points. Adoption of the speech would have committed the resources of the convention to printing and distributing it. More significantly, it would have placed an organized body of free blacks on record in support of the right of the slaves to pick up the gun and seize their freedom. This would have had immediate consequences for the abolitionist movement.

The reaction of the black delegates who objected to the speech was mild compared to that of many white abolitionists. The *Liberator* in its convention coverage labeled Garnet's address "inflammatory," "provocative," and a "flight of fancy." The paper intimated that he had called for "drastic approaches" while safely established in the North out of danger. The *Liberator* took the opportunity to praise the performance of the "Massachusetts delegates" (Douglass, Remond, and others) who were "true to the interests of the slave."[7] In other words those who defended the Garrisonian position were noble and honorable, and men like Garnet and Ray were unscrupulous demagogues. The *Liberator* even attempted to give the impression that Garnet and his supporters had completely rigged the convention against the Garrisonians: "During the debate, Wm. L. Garrison was brought in for his share of abuse."[8]

There were other efforts to discredit Garnet. Two weeks later, the *Liberator* published a lengthy article denouncing Garnet written by Maria Weston Chapman, a poet and abolitionist activist. In her article, Mrs. Chapman displayed much of the racist paternalism that characterized the thinking of white abolitionists. Her main charge against Garnet was that he had fallen under the influence of "bad counsel." This subtle intimation that blacks could not think and act for themselves without the instruction of whites was a rehashing of standard accusations leveled at blacks when they attempted to develop independent organizations and programs.

In a letter,* two months later, Garnet answered Mrs. Chapman's charges:

> You are not the only person who has told your humble servant that his humble productions have been produced by the "*counsel*" of some anglo-saxon. I have expected no more from ignorant slaveholders and their apologists, but I really looked for better things from Mrs. Maria W. Chapman, an anti-slavery poetess, and editor *pro tem.* of the Boston *Liberator*. I can think on the subject of human rights without "counsel," either from men of the West, or the women of the East.[9]

Despite the criticism, Garnet did not relent in his attack on the institutions of oppression. He now firmly believed that violence was the only method through which slavery could be eliminated. He reiterated this several years later

---

* The complete text of this letter is in Appendix Five.

when a group of slaves had been recaptured after an escape attempt:

> The attempted exodus of these poor brethren was un-
> fortunate. They ought to have been better prepared.
> One good cannon, well managed, would have crippled
> a dozen steamers. If white men were to undertake to
> run away from human blood-hounds, they would see
> to it, that the telegraph wires were cut the distance of
> every ten miles, in the direction of their flight. More
> than this they would do; they would pull up the rails
> of the railroads, and stop the speed of the iron horses.
> Do you think . . . it would be an unpardonable sin for
> slaves to do the same ?[10]

Garnet here took the question of violence to its limits.
None of the recognized black abolitionist leaders had dared
speak so boldly. Astutely observing events, he saw that
revolutionary situations were developing in various nations. Blacks, he felt, should keep pace with these trends
and prepare to change American society. In May 1848,
at a meeting of the Society for the Promotion of Education Among Colored Children, Garnet expanded on this
theme:

> This age is a revolutionizing age; the time has been
> when we did not expect to see revolutions; but now
> we expect them, and they are daily passing before our
> eyes; and change after change, and revolution after
> revolution will undoubtedly take place, until all men
> are placed upon equality. Then, and not till then, will
> all enjoy that liberty and equality that God has
> destined us to participate in. (*North Star,* May 19,
> 1848)

Garnet was not the first Northern black to articulate
such beliefs. There were clear precedents for his action.

David Walker in his *Appeal* issued in 1829 had called for the violent destruction of slavery. Walker has been credited with influencing the development of Garnet's radical thought, and to an extent he did. Garnet was thoroughly familiar with Walker's life and work. After receiving permission from Walker's widow, Garnet, in April 1848, published his own address to the Buffalo convention and the *Appeal* together as a pamphlet. (Part of the costs of publication was paid by John Brown.) In the foreword, Garnet contributed a short biographical sketch of Walker's career. He considered the *Appeal* to be the single most important work to come from the pen of a black man. In the preface, he stated, "The work is valuable, because it was among the first, and was actually the boldest and most direct appeal in behalf of freedom, which was made in the early part of the anti-slavery reformation."

Though Walker's *Appeal* received the greatest exposure, it was not the only radical work to have an impact on the thinking of blacks. In 1829 Robert Young published a pamphlet entitled *The Ethiopian Manifesto Issued in Defence of the Blackman's Rights in the Scale of Universal Freedom*. Although Young did not explicitly call for slave rebellions, he did warn:

> Ah! doth your expanding judgment, base slaveholder, not from here descry that the shackles which have been by you so undeservingly forged upon a wretched Ethiopian's frame, are about to be forever from him unlinked? (published by Robert Young in New York City, 1829).

In 1837, Samuel Cornish, in the introduction to a series of articles by William Whipper on the abolitionist movement published in the *Colored American*, wrote: "But we honestly confess that we have yet to learn what virtue there would be in using moral weapons, in defense against kidnappers or a midnight incendiary with a torch in his hand." Four years later David Ruggles, leader of the New York Vigilance Committee, urged in a call he issued for a convention:

> Strike for freedom, or die slaves! In our cause, mere words are nothing—action is everything. Buckle on your armor, and appear at the convention, remembering that our cause demands of us union and agitation —agitation and action.[11]

Obviously Garnet's ideas were not formed in a vacuum. His speech directly reflected the attitudes of the black masses. Despite the fact that the masses were not represented in the councils of the anti-slavery societies, they constituted a growing force and had to be reckoned with. Many blacks had escaped from slavery and were not prepared to submit to any form of injustice without fighting back. For the most part they lacked the formal education of many of the black abolitionist leaders. Employed mainly as unskilled laborers, the black masses knew violence, often from firsthand experience. They were not as likely to refrain from using it as the abolitionists were. Their mere presence injected militancy into the black movement, which was both dynamic and progressive. Garnet was probably influenced by many of the fugitive slaves whom he had aided while assisting the underground railroad in New York. Generally, runaways were willing to kill or die rather than return to slavery.

Circumstances forced Garnet and the younger blacks to pay attention to the sentiments of the black masses. In Garnet's 1843 address to the Buffalo convention the flowery phrases and clichés usually present in the speeches of the abolitionist leaders are not to be found. It was a document of fact.

Garnet was not the first black to openly call for a mass slave rebellion, but the impact of his speech was more profound than that of previous declarations because he forcefully expressed an ideal that was beginning to gain acceptance within the black communities of the North. Further, Garnet spoke before a national assemblage and therefore received maximum attention by the general public. The convention's failure to adopt the speech was not really important. The fact that it was presented and seriously discussed legitimized it. The main measure of its value, however, was its overall effect on the actions of blacks.

In the years immediately following, nearly every meeting of free blacks passed a resolution affirming belief in independent action. The Michigan Negro Convention in October 1843 called for blacks to wage "unceasing war" against tyranny. In 1844, Moses Dickson formed a secret organization known as the "international order of Twelve of the Knights and Daughters of Tabor." The avowed intention of this group was to overthrow slavery by any means. Rev. Henry Johnson, at the Colored Suffrage Convention in New York in 1845, said that "the colored population were ready to take the musket, if necessary, to defend our churches, our family associations, and the rights of their neighbors."

After 1845, the trends Garnet set in motion at the Buffalo convention were accelerated. Blacks gathering at Boston and Portland, Maine, in 1848 passed spirited resolutions urging the total end to slavery by force if necessary. A convention meeting in Detroit in 1849 passed similar resolutions.

In 1850, the Fugitive Slave Convention, meeting in New York, in its "Address to the Fugitives" labeled the slaves "prisoners of war in an enemy's country." The address called upon the slaves to begin a campaign of destruction against the plantations: "If your oppressors have rights of property, you, at least, are exempt from all obligation to respect them. . . . By all the rules of war, you have the fullest liberty to plunder, burn and kill."

The Ohio State Convention in 1850 demanded that oppressed blacks "strike the first blow" for freedom. Under the leadership of Charles Langston, the outspoken secretary of the Ohio Anti-Slavery Society, the convention passed a series of resolutions condemning colonization, opposing the payment of taxes, advocating physical resistance to slave kidnapers, appealing for black unity, and promoting the establishment of a black press. Another resolution stated:

> Resolved, That we still adhere to the doctrine of urging the slave to leave immediately with his hoe on his shoulder, for a land of liberty, and would accordingly recommend that five hundred copies of Walker's *Appeal,* and Henry H. Garnet's *Address to the Slaves* be obtained in the name of the Convention, and gratuitously circulated.

Convention resolutions were not the only manifestations of the new spirit of self-assertion. Some conservative black leaders were compelled to rethink their positions on the question of slave rebellions. Douglass, for one, shocked an anti-slavery audience in Boston in June 1849 when he remarked:

> I should welcome the intelligence tomorrow, should it come, that the slaves had risen in the South, and that the sable arms which had been engaged in beautifying and adorning the South, were engaged in spreading death and devastation.[12]

Douglass' speech was a departure from the ideological stance of the Garrisonians. Another Garrison stalwart, Remond, several years later commended the action of three blacks who had killed their former master:

> It is ours to point to Attucks, of by-gone days; and we could, if we would, point to Freeman, and Parker, and Jackson of Christiana celebrity; for if Washington and Attucks opened the revolution of the past, Parker, and Jackson, and Freeman, opened the revolution of

the present, when they shot down Gorsuch and his son at Christiana.[13]

Garnet's speech, a milestone in the abolitionist movement, ranks as one of the major documents of the entire pre–Civil War period. William McAdoo, in his *Pre–Civil War Black Nationalism,* states that Garnet's address ushered in the era of revolutionary nationalism and "undermined the corrupt role of those white liberal managers in black conventions and in other gatherings of black people" (*PL Magazine,* July–August 1966, p. 29). Closer to the scene. James McCune Smith, an active participant in the conventions of the 1840's, said this "document elicited more discussion than any other paper brought before that or any other deliberate body of colored persons and their friends."[14]

After 1843, blacks were in complete command of the affairs of their organizations. The 1847 national Negro convention is undoubtedly the best illustration of this.

Most of the prominent figures in the black movement assembled at the convention, held at Garnet's Liberty Street Presbyterian Church in October 1847. Douglass, Brown, Smith, Ray, Nell, Pennington, Beman, Crummell, and, of course, Garnet were among the sixty-seven delegates present at the opening session in Troy. Garnet read the convention call and nominated Peyton Harris of New York for convention president. Garnet was then elected to the rules and the business committees.

From his position on the rules committee, he laid down thirteen rules that would govern convention procedure. The most important of these made it mandatory that all resolutions be approved by the business committee before consideration by the convention. Those who served on this committee were in a position not only to shape policy but also to control the direction of the convention.

The opening proposals were for the establishment of a bank and a national press, both under the "control of the people of color." Garnet supported the proposal for a national press, arguing that it was one of "the most successful means which can be used for the overthrow of slavery and caste in this country." He added: "The establishment of a national Printing Press would send terror into the ranks of our enemies, and encourage all our friends, whose friendship is greater than their selfishness" (Minutes of the 1847 Convention). Garnet saw the press as a practical means to promote "the doctrine of self help." This proposal was opposed by both Brown and Douglass, who felt that blacks should support black newspapers, such as the *Ram's Horn*, the *National Watchman*, and the *North Star*, already in operation. After further discussion, the proposal was adopted. Garnet was appointed "home agent" for the press. Returning to an idea put forth in Buffalo in 1843, the convention recommended that a committee be appointed to supervise the paper.

The education committee, chaired by Crummell, proposed the creation of a college for blacks. Garnet, though, was against this. He believed a black college was unnecessary because some colleges did admit blacks. As an alternative, he favored the establishment of black academies. However, when submitted as a resolution, the committee's proposal was approved by the convention.

On the second day, Garnet was invited by the convention chairman to deliver his "Address to the Slaves." This time the response of the delegates was overwhelmingly enthusiastic. There was no discussion of the once-controversial speech.

Later, Douglass, representing the committee upon the "Best Means to Abolish Slavery and Caste in the United States," presented a report. Garnet opposed its adoption because it contained the phrases "sanctity of religion," "shedding of blood," and "moral suasion." On this issue, Garnet had the support of a majority of the delegates. Willis Hodges, John Spence, and James Gardner gave speeches backing his position. The report was then forced back into committee for modification. When it was presented again, Garnet again objected, suggesting that if "moral suasion" had to be retained in the wording, then "and political action" should be added after it. In the absence of a compromise, the report was defeated when put to convention vote.

Meanwhile, the business committee had been carefully considering the bank proposal. To determine the prospects of such an enterprise, R. D. Kenny provided the committee with statistics on banking and commerce. Satisfied that a bank could be founded, the committee offered the following resolution:

> Resolved, That the creation and permanent establishment of a Banking Institution by the colored people of the United States is a measure which deserves the attention of this Convention.[15]

Thomas Van Rensselaer, a committee member, thought that such an institution was necessary "among the colored people of the United States, because they at present contribute to their own degradation by investing capital in the hands of their 'enemies.'" Garnet and several other delegates were not convinced. They could not see the feasibility of blacks' establishing a bank without capital and firmly developed sources of community revenue. The majority of the delegates, thinking otherwise, approved the resolution.

The final resolutions adopted by the convention called for committees "to report on the propriety of establishing a Printing Establishment and Press for the colored people of the United States" and the "wants of Educational privileges of the colored people in the United States." They also advocated temperance, local efforts for self-development, opposition to racism in the church, the destruction of slavery, and, most importantly:

> Resolved, That this convention recommend to our people the propriety of instructing their sons in the art of war.[16]

The main thrust of the convention could be seen in the final reports issued by the committees. The one on the national press concluded:

> Let there be, then, in these United States, a Printing Press, a copious supply of type, a full and complete establishment, wholly controlled by colored men; let the thinking writing-man, the compositors, pressman, printers' help, all, all be men of color;—then let there come from said establishment a weekly periodical and a quarterly periodical, edited as well as printed by colored men;—let this establishment be so well endowed as to be beyond the chances of temporary patronage; and then there will be a fixed fact, a rallying point, towards which the strong and the weak amongst us would look with confidence and hope; from which would flow a steady stream of comfort and exhortation to the weary strugglers, and burning rebuke and overwhelming argument upon those who dare impede our way.[17]

The committee on commerce adapted its report from the Jamaica Hamic Association, a group in the West Indies that was attempting to open trade links with Africa. The committee resolved to work closely with this organization in order to establish "a more intimate acquaintance with our brethren in those islands."

The committee on agriculture called for increased ownership of land as a means of gaining economic independence. It included in its report a special resolution commending Gerrit Smith for his donations of land for black settlement. The cultivation of this land was seen as a step toward "placing in the hands of the oppressed the means of self-elevation."

Falling in line with the mood of the convention, Douglass' committee in its report eliminated the term "moral suasion" and urged blacks "to *agitate! agitate!! agitate!!!* till our rights are restored."

Clearly the delegates to this convention were concerned with devising programs to increase black self-determination. The resolutions centered around the real needs of Northern blacks. There was a marked absence of the rhetoric that had tended to characterize previous conventions. The delegates did not get sidetracked into debates over abstractions such as freedom and justice. Reports were precisely worded so as not to cause any confusion over goals. An intense feeling of cooperation among the delegates was shown in the proceedings. The convention was a product of the combined resources of the participants. It received almost no publicity in the regular commercial press and only scattered notices in the abolitionist press. As a result, the convention was, in every sense, a genuine black convention.

The resolutions, though never completely implemented, did encourage local initiative by blacks. Several black periodicals, stemming from the idea of a national press, began to be published shortly after the convention. Douglass formed the *North Star* in December 1847.* He was so absorbed by the thought of publishing that he wrote an article expressing disappointment that the resolutions for a national press had not been sent to him at the *North Star*. Douglass now sincerely believed that blacks should "unite in sustaining the colored periodicals already in existence."

The principle of self-help that the convention strongly endorsed became a major concern of Garnet's during the next few years. In 1848, he moved from Troy to Geneva, New York, where he became pastor of the local black church and instructor at its school. While there, he worked to strengthen both the church and the school as institutions within the black community. In an article on blacks in western New York, he declared:

* Garrison, opposing the formation of the *North Star*, labeled Douglass' action "impulsive," "inconsiderate," and "highly inconsistent." Before this, Garrison had stood against Cornish when he announced plans to publish the *Colored American*.

Self-help—This principle is invincible. Regard it either in a moral, physical, or intellectual light, it is to an oppressed people what Moses was to the Hebrews—what Virginius was to Rome, and what Toussaint L'Ouverture was to his golden island of the ocean.

My heart leaps with joy as I behold my long-suffering and noble people laying aside their old garments of dependence, and entering upon their own work.[18]

In the same article, Garnet set forth many of his criticisms of the white Christian church. Religion was central to Garnet's existence. He was well aware that the black church was quite different from the white church. As he increased his attacks on the latter, he became more supportive of the former.

CHAPTER FOUR

Racism, Religion, and the Black Struggle

As a minister, Garnet saw in the black church many of black society's strengths and weaknesses. From the 1820's on, the black church occupied a dominant position in Northern black communities. Before the Civil War, the church performed a needed function within the organized life of free blacks. It was the center of many activities, and often it was the only established agency in the community capable of generating any social movement.

Many black churchmen felt it their duty to devise programs to meet the pressing needs of free blacks. W. E. B. Du Bois notes: "The Negro churches were the birth places of Negro schools and of all agencies which seek to promote the intelligence of the masses. . . . Consequently all movements for social betterment are apt to center in the churches."[1] As racism became firmly entrenched in the North, black churches began to house abolitionist gatherings. To combat oppression, the churches actively sought to stimulate social consciousness among their congregations.

In Philadelphia in the late 1700's, Richard Allen and Absalom Jones, both black ministers, initiated a drive to create independent religious institutions within the city's black community. Their efforts resulted in the formation of the African Methodist Episcopal Church in 1816. In other cities, African societies were organized in conjunction with the A.M.E. Church. In the other religious denominations, blacks also founded churches along separate lines.

The A.M.E. Church, being the largest black denomination, took the lead in the freedom movement. It sponsored societies to promote the purchase of free produce and the use of free labor, both of which were considered harmful to slavery. In Philadelphia, the church formed an African society for mutual relief to dispense food and clothes to the black poor. By 1830, the black church had begun to provide some direction to abolitionism. This was reflected in the convention movement. Eight black ministers, including Garnet and Ray, were listed as founders of the American and Foreign Anti-Slavery Society in 1840.

However, all black ministers were not progressive—particularly those who had gained economic status. Many ministers were cool toward the abolitionist movement. They often refused the use of their churches for anti-slavery meetings. Young blacks were openly critical of the practices of these churches. The Garrisonians opposed religion in general because they believed the church, black and white, imbued blacks with the notion that prayer and patience were the solutions to injustice. Many churches objected to any political action by the oppressed.

In the South, blacks were originally forbidden to hold religious meetings and to read the Bible. Gradually this changed as time passed. Clever planters sought every means to manipulate and regulate the lives of their slaves. They came to regard the church as a safety valve for the channeling of black resentment into harmless escapism. William Wells Brown, who spent much of his youth in slavery, commented on the distorted relation between religion and the plantation:

> It was not uncommon in St. Louis to pass by an auction-stand, and behold a woman upon the auction-block, and hear the seller crying out, "How much is offered for this woman? She is a good cook, good

washer, a good obedient servant. She has got religion!"
Why should this man tell the purchasers that she has
religion? I answer, because in Missouri, and as far as
I have any knowledge of slavery in the other States,
the religious teaching consists in teaching the slave
that he must never strike a white man; that God made
him for a slave; and that, when whipped, he must not
find fault,—for the Bible says, "He that knoweth his
master's will, and doeth it not, shall be beaten with
many stripes!" And slaveholders find such religion
very profitable to them.[2]

Garnet was thoroughly against this misuse of religion.
He agreed with the Garrisonians that the white church
was supporting slavery and racism and that many black
churches were reactionary and slowed down the struggle.
Garnet, though, stopped short of completely indicting
Christianity. He attempted to distinguish between the
practices of the church and the precepts of theology.
  While on a lecture tour of Rhode Island and Connecticut
in 1845, he visited many of the churches in the area. He
noted that many blacks were becoming lax in their attendance at church. Garnet blamed the church rather than
the people for this attitude:

The manner in which they are treated in many places
by the prejudice which is tolerated by the church,
drives them out from all public worship, and a most
fruitful source of infidelity is opened. With a heart
deeply affected I tell the American church wherever
it tolerates caste—that it is doing more than all other
things to drive the colored people into downright
infidelity.[3]

During a stop in New London, Connecticut, he took the
opportunity to observe how the churches there treated
blacks. He was forced to conclude:

Every church in the city, excepting the Roman Catholic, tolerates caste of the most wicked kind. The intelligent colored people cannot, nor ought not to endure this treatment. Many Christians stay at home —and for this they are called infidels—and many impenitent are actually shut out of the kingdom of heaven. Great God! where will these churches stand in the judgement?[4]

The only real vestiges of racial tolerance that he could find "were among the sailors."

Garnet felt that blacks should develop their own churches. This would be the best way to ensure that blacks got any meaning out of worship. However, Garnet was not willing to compromise on his criticism of white religious leaders. He demanded that they assume responsibility for the practices of their churches and begin to live up to the ideals of truth and justice supposedly embodied in the basic tenets of Christianity.

At an anti-slavery convention in Philadelphia in October 1848, he repeated this theme. In his address to the gathering, he called upon blacks to sever any remaining ties they might have with the "pro-slavery churches."[5] A report drafted by the committee he chaired strongly condemned the churches in America as the "bulwark of slavery." The committee recommended that

their brethren henceforth exclude slaveholders and their apologists from their pulpits; to withdraw their support from the American Board of Foreign Missions and Bible and Tract societies, all of which in this country, are pro-slavery, and use your pecuniary means for the promotion of your religious institutions, which are clear of blood-guiltiness.[6]

This report received the convention's enthusiastic approval and apparently mirrored the general sentiments of the blacks in the city, where the A.M.E. Church had a strong and well-organized following.

Garnet's actions were always determined by the needs of the anti-slavery movement. His concern that blacks have the benefit of religious training was based on his belief that it was a requisite for building character, strength, and discipline. Viewing religion as something that could serve mankind, he meant to employ it as a vehicle for black self-expression and uplift. Garnet wanted to reconcile theory and practice in the church. One without the other was meaningless. His goal was to utilize the church in the liberation struggle. Devotion to God was equated with devotion to the struggle.* In Garnet's eyes there was never a dichotomy between the two:

> This church that has torn us, must help to heal; she who has scattered, must help to gather; and both of these things we must do ourselves. I totally despair of my people's redemption until we trust more in God and labor more in our own cause.[7]

This distinctive feature of black religion was undoubtedly a cultural carry-over from West Africa, where

---

* The desire to put God in the service of the black movement was given much space in the writings of numerous black ministers. For example, Pennington, a Presbyterian minister, wrestled with this idea in his autobiography, *The Fugitive Blacksmith:*

In the spring of 1829, I found my mind unusually perplexed about the state of the slave. I was enjoying rare privileges in attending a Sabbath school; the great value of Christian knowledge began to be impressed upon my mind to an extent that I had not been conscious of before. I began to contrast my condition with that of ten brothers and sisters I had left in slavery, and the condition of children I saw sitting around me on the Sabbath, with their pious teachers, with that of 700,000 now 800,400 slave children, who had no means of Christian instruction.

the concept of God was never abstract but always prag-
matic. Religion was a useful extension of the needs of
tribal society. Where tribal economy was dependent on
fishing, as in Dahomey, Africans prayed to the gods of the
river; where the dependence was on farming, there were
gods of the soil to whom prayers were offered. The role of
the Afro-American minister often paralleled that of the
traditional tribal priests. The Atlanta study on the Negro
Church stresses this:

> the vast power of the priest in the African state has
> already been noted; his realm alone—the province of
> religion and medicine—remained largely unaffected
> by the plantation system in many important particu-
> lars. The Negro priest, therefore, early became an
> important figure . . . and found his function as the
> interpreter of the supernatural, the comforter of the
> sorrowing, and as the one who expressed, rudely, but
> picturesquely, the longing and disappointment and
> resentment of a stolen people.[8]

During the early part of 1849, Garnet spent considerable
time attempting to organize a Christian convention. He
wanted it to cut across both "caste and sectarian lines." He
hoped such a convention would form a "permanent state
society" that would employ agents to encourage blacks to
unite in a program for group advancement. Garnet offered
to correspond with anyone interested in his proposal. Apparently, few people were. The convention never material-
ized, and Garnet turned his attention to other matters.

Garnet's speeches were sprinkled with religious allu-
sions. His 1843 speech to the Buffalo convention contains
many examples. He intertwined references to the Bible and
the black struggle:

> —To such degradation it is sinful in the extreme for
>   you to make voluntary submission.

—Liberty is a spirit sent out from God, and like its great Author, is no respecter of persons.

—Neither God, nor angels, or just men, command you to suffer for a single moment.

—From the first moment that you breathed the air of heaven, you have been accustomed to nothing but hardship.

Other blacks within the movement also used biblical verses, scripture, and especially spirituals. Harriet Tubman used lines in the spirituals such as "When that there old chariot comes, I'm going to leave you; I'm bound for the promised land," to signal her coming and to convey messages to the slaves about escape. After uprisings or slave conspiracies, such as Denmark Vessey's, the black church was often banned by the planters in the immediate area.

Religion and its place in the black struggle was debated by black abolitionists. At a meeting in May 1849, Garnet, Ward, Douglass, and Remond engaged in a four-way discussion on the question of whether abolitionists should send Bibles to the slaves. Garnet defended the idea, sharply rebuking Douglass for stating that the Bible made slaves unhappy. He saw no contradiction in the slaves' studying the Bible while preparing to liberate themselves. Garnet thought that the two activities were parallel.

Garnet had become a public figure. A leader among blacks, he was known to many people active in the abolitionist movement abroad. In the early part of 1850, Garnet accepted an invitation from the English Friends of Free Labor to visit in England. He considered the trip an opportunity to gain foreign support for blacks' struggles in America.

CHAPTER FIVE

Internationalizing
the Struggle

By the late 1840's, the free labor movement in England
had attracted support from a large section of the working
class there. The movement, initiated by abolitionists, was
an outgrowth of reaction to slavery. Many anti-slavery
proponents along with the workers had banded together
to boycott all products made by slaves. The industrial revolution in Europe had made English workers realize that
chattel slavery undercut wages and restricted the market
for free labor. The institution of slavery threatened both
the livelihood and the status of English workers.

Free labor advocates demanded the complete abolition
of slavery. This demand was backed by many British industrialists, who calculated that a stable labor force would
increase their profits and be less likely to stir up trouble.

Supporters of this movement had long maintained relations with abolitionists in America. They considered it
advantageous to aid the anti-slavery struggle there, and
they believed that having Garnet in England would
strengthen ties between the movements on both sides of
the ocean. The arrangements for Garnet's trip were han-
dled by the famed English abolitionist Mrs. Henry Rich-
ardson. Arriving in England early in the summer of 1850,
Garnet took up residence in Newcastle upon Tyne. Immediately, he embarked on a tour, lecturing to small groups
connected with the free labor cause.

While in England, Garnet became interested in the activities of the international peace movement. The peace campaign had already enlisted the support of black abolitionists such as Douglass, Pennington, and Brown. Brown had attended the World Peace Congress in Paris in 1849 as a representative of the American Peace Society. Similar congresses were held in London and Brussels in the same year.

Many American abolitionists gave unqualified backing to the peace movement. They saw the relationship between war and slavery: both were products of the same aggressive, expansionist system. This recognition prompted many leading figures in the anti-slavery societies to join peace societies that had been formed in America.*

The peace congress sponsors planned to hold another gathering in Frankfurt am Main, Germany, in August 1850. They wanted it to be the largest and to attract as much international support as possible. In August Garnet left England to attend. He was slated to serve as an official American delegate. The American delegation consisted of thirty persons, mostly abolitionists. One of them, Joshua Giddings, had supported, from his seat in the United States Congress, a petition by the citizens of Oberlin, Ohio, to the government for "a national vessel to transport delegates to the peace congress in Germany."[1]

Garnet's presence at the congress elicited a great deal of excitement from both representatives and journalists. One reporter observed: "[His] appearance, he being of pure negro blood, excited considerable sensation and interest."[2]

At the first session, Garnet and two other delegates spoke in favor of a resolution, which read:

* The New England Resistance Society, organized in 1838 by Garrison and other Boston abolitionists, pledged its members to nonparticipation in all wars. No group, however, was more vocal in its denunciation of the war than Northern blacks. They correctly saw war as an expansionist move by American slave interests. Douglass called it an act of plunder and "wholesale murder" by the American government.

The Congress of the Friends of Universal Peace, assembled at Frankfurt-on-the-Main, on the 22nd, 23rd
and 24th of August, 1850, acknowledges that recourse
to arms being condemned alike by religion, morality,
reason, and humanity, it is the duty of all men to
adopt measures calculated to abolish war; and the
Congress recommends all its members to labour in
their respective countries by means of a better education of youth, by the pulpit, the platform, and the
press, as well as by other practical methods, to eradicate those hereditary hatreds and political and commercial prejudices which have been so generally the
cause of disastrous wars.[3]

Garnet praised the work of those in the peace movement
and announced that blacks in America were in general
accord with their aims. He urged all to come together for
the future of humanity. Garnet indicated that Germans
could best help the anti-slavery struggle by forming "free
labor stores" throughout their country.

Many of the delegates realized that it would take more
than eloquent appeals and lofty resolutions to end war.
Idealism alone could not sustain the peace movement at
the very moment that the nations of Western Europe were
preparing to undertake a mission of imperialist conquest
against the nonwhite people of Asia and Africa. Militarism
had become part of the fabric of these nations. It determined their diplomatic policies.

The peace movement received a cool reception from
national governments. It failed to grow and win the support of those in power. The London Peace Congress of 1851
was the final attempt to muster the forces of peace. As the
fight against slavery intensified in the 1850's, American
abolitionists found less time to devote to the peace movement.

After the congress in Frankfurt, Garnet traveled through
Bavaria, Prussia, and France, lecturing. He was accom-
panied by Joseph Sturge, an English abolitionist who had

been instrumental in organizing the first World Anti-Slavery Convention in 1840 and the international peace congresses.

When he returned to England, Garnet divided his time between lecturing and delivering sermons in many of the country's leading churches. While in Newcastle, he received the news that the United States Congress had enacted the Fugitive Slave Act. This represented the final capitulation of the national government to the Southern planters.

The act, passed in September 1850 as part of the so-called compromise of 1850, was designed to stop the increasing flow of runaway slaves to the North. This exodus cost the South millions of dollars a year in property and labor. The law was sweeping: it required all whites to "aid and assist" in the capture of "fugitives." There were no provisions for trials, only for a hearing before a federal judge or a specially appointed commissioner. Northern blacks were, of course, shocked and angered by the act. Hardly any black leaders would now caution blacks against violence. Blacks were nearly unanimously in favor of using physical force to resist the law.

J. W. Loguen exclaimed:

I don't respect this law—I don't fear it—I won't obey it! It outlaws me, and I outlaw it, and the men who attempt to enforce it on me. I place the governmental officials on the ground that they place me. I will not live a slave, and if force is employed to re-enslave me, I shall make preparations to meet the crisis as becomes a man.[4]

Sam R. Ward wrote: "it throws us back upon the natural and inalienable right of self-defence—self-protection. . . . Let the men who would execute this bill beware."[5]

Douglass said: "The only way to make the Fugitive Slave Law a dead letter is to make half a dozen or more dead kidnappers."[6]

Garnet held a similar view. Writing from Newcastle, he implored blacks to resist the law and "act like men." He warned:

There are a few men in America who will not acquiesce in this enactment. This extreme measure will hasten the downfall of slavery. Knowing the spirit of my people, I do not hesitate to say that the law can never, never be enforced.[7]

He also remarked that British public opinion was firmly against the act. At the meetings where he spoke, he urged resistance.

In December 1850, he began an extensive lecture tour of Ireland and Scotland. Throughout January he made daily appearances, addressing crowds at public meetings. In Belfast Garnet spoke before that city's anti-slavery society. Immediately afterward, the society passed a resolution condemning the Fugitive Slave Act. In Ballymoney, Garnet delivered a lecture at the Primitive Methodist Church on slavery and religion. He praised the churches in Ireland for their efforts in the struggle and remarked that "some of the most distinguished Bishops of the Primitive Christian Church were black men."[8] He questioned the sincerity of critics who regarded him as "too violent." He was followed by Rev. John L. Rentoul, who assured him that he had the solid support and respect of the Irish people. Rentoul described the welcome Garnet received:

you will permit me to say that the visit of Mr. Garnet to Ballymoney was hailed with the greatest enthusiasm—several gentlemen greeted him on his arrival, with an Irish welcome. On the Sabbath, he preached twice in my church to crowded and delighted congregations; on the evening of the Sabbath, we had to admit by ticket, at sixpence each. On Monday evening, we entertained him at a soiree when near 600 persons sat down to tea. Ten Presbyterian ministers were present to give him the right hand of fellowship.[9]

Rentoul, carried away by the spirit of the moment, invited Garnet and his family to come to Ireland to live. There he would be treated as a champion of the freedom struggle.

Garnet returned to Belfast several days later and spoke at a public meeting on "the relation which the churches of America bear to slavery." After his speech a resolution was adopted deploring the "inconsistent conduct of professing Christian ministers and laymen, in upholding an iniquitous system, so contrary to the precepts and spirit of the Gospel."[10]

Garnet continued his lectures for the next few days. He put in appearances at anti-slavery gatherings all over the Belfast area. At one meeting, a resolution was passed insisting that British churches pressure religious leaders in America to separate themselves from slaveholders. After a brief stop in Scotland, Garnet returned to England. The London *Times* reported that he remained in great demand as a speaker. Garnet's impact on the British public did not escape the attention of American abolitionists. Samuel Rhodes, a noted abolitionist, in a letter to Gerrit Smith wrote: "H. H. Garnet has made a glorious beginning in England and I shall regret it if he precipitatively abandons the field."[11]

That Garnet found fertile ground in Britain for his abolitionist message was not surprising. Douglass, Pennington, and Brown, along with recently escaped slaves such as William and Ellen Craft and Moses Grandy, all had been greatly acclaimed when they toured the country. Ward, who followed Garnet to England in 1851, mentioned this in his *Autobiography of a Fugitive Negro:*

It was with the greatest delight that I found in every part of England, Ireland, Scotland, and Wales, that abolitionism is not a mere abstract idea, but a practi-

cal question of grave importance. It is not because, to
a certain extent, anti-slavery sentiments are fashion-
able and natural, that these persons approve them,
but because of their intrinsic character.

In May 1851, Garnet joined Horace Greeley and other
notables in addressing a massive temperance and anti-
slavery meeting at London's Exeter Hall. The following
month, he, Crummell, and Brown were present at the
World Anti-Slavery Convention held in London. As the
official American delegate, Garnet delivered an address
to the convention. He continued to make the rounds. In
June he was the featured speaker at a convention sponsored by the Congregation Union of England. In ministe-
rial prose, he stated: "If we are to benefit the oppressed,
it must not be by diluting the waters of justice, but by
preserving them in their purity, and declaring the truth
in unmistakable language" (*Pennsylvania Freeman,* July 3,
1851).

Garnet's schedule was so packed with engagements that
he felt compelled to apologize to a correspondent for not
keeping those in America abreast of his activities. He
worried about the welfare of his family. When his wife
became pregnant with their third child, he had left her in
Geneva while he made the trip. Receiving much praise but
very little money for his lectures, he was unable to send
much money to his family. Before he had left Geneva,
Garnet had advised his wife to contact Gerrit Smith for
assistance in the event of financial emergency. When both
of her sons became ill in December 1850 (one of them,
James Cromwell Garnet, later died), she appealed to Smith
for money. Apparently she had not received the money
Garnet had sent to her on board a steamer from Liverpool. She explained to Smith that she had written to
Europe about the money but had not received an answer.
Mrs. Garnet also told Smith that she had gotten some
money from another source but that it was not adequate
to meet her expenses. Smith came to her aid. He was able

to raise enough money to send her and their children to England to join Garnet.

In November, Garnet went to Scotland, where he lectured at meetings in Glasgow sponsored by local industrialists. In Edinburgh, he spoke to rallies held under the auspices of the Ladies' Negro Emancipation Society. Always his words were the same. The laws of America had made more than three million people slaves and had transformed through the Fugitive Slave Act every citizen into a slave catcher and kidnaper. He would end his speech with praise for blacks and others for their defiance of the law.

After speeches in several more towns, he arrived back in Newcastle, where the citizens greeted him with a gala anti-slavery soiree. The four hundred people present closed the evening by passing four resolutions. The first three condemned the American church and slavery. The fourth called for a boycott of American products:

> Seeing that the great design of the Fugitive Slave Act is to supply the markets of the world, and, above all, British markets, with slave produce, in competition with free labour, this meeting would earnestly recommend to their friends the *Free Labor Movement,* as a legitimate and effectual method of putting down a system of wickedness such as can find no parallel on the face of the earth.[12]

The resolution showed that Garnet and the English free labor advocates were completely aware of the economic foundations of slavery. In their proposals was little of the moralistic sentimentality usually found in resolutions offered by American abolitionists. They were not far off in their estimate that if the cessation of trade between merchants and the planters eliminated a few markets, more damage would be done to slavery than had been accomplished by all the appeals and declarations put together.

Garnet paid close attention to events in America. He noted with pleasure acts of resistance by blacks and abolitionists. In some instances whole communities had risen to protect the rights of blacks accused of being fugitives, even to the point of rescuing them from the snatches of the slave catchers.

The government, though, did not stand still. Where it could, it retaliated with stiff penalties for infringement of the Fugitive Slave Act. Garnet was particularly angered by the jailing of his friend William L. Chaplain, a Massachusetts lawyer who had helped a slave to escape. From Newcastle, Garnet wrote an article hailing Chaplain for his deed and demanding his release. He said that he wanted to inform the English public there about the facts of the case and assure them that Chaplain enjoyed the support of "millions of bondsmen, who will pronounce their blessings upon him while his name shall be often repeated in the anthems of the free."[13]

While working with the free labor movement, Garnet joined the West India Committee, formed to coordinate the activities of those who were promoting "the use of free-labour produce instead of that raised by the labour of slaves." The main focus of the committee's attention was the British colonies in the Caribbean. Garnet tried to enlist support for the group. To explain the program of the committee, Garnet had to acquaint himself with the history of the West Indies. This increased his desire to live and work there.

At the end of 1852, he became affiliated with the United Presbyterian Church of Scotland and was commissioned by the church to go to Jamaica as a missionary and teacher. He was given the pastorship of the local Presbyterian church in Stirling, Grange Hill, located not far from Kingston. Garnet and his wife left England in December 1852 and arrived in Kingston in late January. He began a series of lectures on the "origins and implications of the Fugitive Slave Law."

For the first time, Garnet was in a country where the

majority of the population was black. He observed that many blacks owned land and exercised some control over local affairs. Tremendously impressed, he envisioned opportunities for black development in Jamaica that did not exist, given the differing circumstances of black life, in America.

In June 1853, he addressed a letter to various newspapers in America in an attempt to recruit seventy blacks to work on the estates of two of his parishioners. The rate of pay would be $2.50 for each acre of cane cleared. The grower was willing to parcel out his land in shares to the workers for further cultivation. The principal crops that could be grown and marketed were rice, Indian corn, and tobacco. As an added inducement, Garnet listed the schools in the area in which blacks could receive a regular common school education, with special instruction in Greek and Latin. He also mentioned that the landholders were sincerely concerned about the welfare of the masses and that they "would do all in their power to promote the happiness of their hands."[14]

Preference would be given to those who were experienced in farm work. There was, however, a limited need for blacksmiths, carpenters, and masons. Garnet hastened to add that blacks who decided to come should not expect Jamaica to be a utopia. He considered the social condition of the working class to be generally worse than in America. The main reasons for this were that "provisions are high, and the roads are bad." Nonetheless, he was convinced that American blacks could make greater strides toward self-development in Jamaica than they could elsewhere.

According to Garnet, the growers desired American blacks because they possessed industry, skills, and "go-ahead enterprise." To facilitate emigration, he sent out copies of the American laws governing travel. He expressed the hope that those who accepted the offer would take no expense money from the British colonial government and would provide their own transportation. In this way they would not be bound to work on the estates for a required amount of time and would "maintain an independence that they otherwise could not do."[15]

Garnet's recruitment efforts did not signify on his part any particular interest, at this point, in emigration as a solution to black oppression in America. He considered emigration an outlet for selected individuals who had skills. Douglass, though, saw it differently. In an article in response to Garnet's letter, he countered that blacks with skills were needed more in America than in any other country:

> The kind of colored men Mr. Garnett [*sic*] wants in Jamaica, are like himself, a part of the life-blood of colored America; and we are opposed to its being drained off either to Canada, Jamaica, or Liberia. . . . Mr. Garnett [*sic*] himself had better come home. He, and men like him, can do more good here than any-where else in the world. For ourselves we can say our home shall be somewhere on the borders of America, unless driven out by bayonets or starvation.[16]

Garnet, unshaken, was content to remain in Jamaica. He began an exhaustive study of the land and people of the island. In a lengthy letter to friends in England, he sum-marized the information he had collected on the character and substance of Jamaican society.* Included was his analysis of the land question, the laboring classes, religion, the plantation system, education, and the racism of the whites. Garnet saw the increasing ownership of land by blacks as an indication of blacks' economic self-suffi-ciency. He deplored the attempts of the white planters to prevent blacks from obtaining fertile land:

> The planters generally believe that to encourage them [blacks] to become landowners would place them in a position of independence, and they are not encouraged

* The complete text of this letter is in Appendix Six.

in their efforts to become owners of the soil. If they buy land it is generally that which is the poorest, and which is not valuable to the planters.[17]

He was equally concerned over the exploitation of the workers by a large number of planters. He warned of a pending social crisis if this condition was not alleviated:

> There is no such thing as a change in wages. The planter fixes the amount and he is the sole judge and arbiter in the matter—and the almost universal opinion of the planters is that to give the people more wages would be tempting them to do less work. The working people, in their turn, affirm that at the present low rate of wages they can do better to cultivate their provision grounds, which with less labour will yield them a better return. . . . This unphilosophical mode of procedure may be satisfactory to both classes for a season, but a crisis must ultimately arise which will prove disastrous to both.[18]

Though satisfied with his work, the feeling always lingered with Garnet that perhaps he was too removed from the main scene of struggle, America. In private correspondence, he expressed this uneasiness: "But alas; when I hear the din of battle coming over from the shores of America my soul leaps up within me."[19] This thought, combined with an eight-month bout with fever, served to cut his stay in Jamaica shorter than he had originally planned. In February 1856, Garnet and his wife and children sailed for Boston. Arriving in March, he was invited to deliver a series of lectures on "Jamaica in Slavery and in Freedom."

Unsure of his plans, Garnet first considered a brief lecture tour of New England and western New York and then a return to Jamaica. Carefully surveying conditions, however, he decided that the struggle in America was pressing. In a letter to Smith, he said that he had been well received in the past and saw no reason why his views would not be supported in the anti-slavery movement. He desired to become "a missionary of liberty." Above all, he wanted to return to his first love, the pulpit. He made it clear, though, that he did not want to be associated with the pro-slavery church.[20] Later in 1856, he accepted the pastorship of the Shiloh Presbyterian Church in New York City, filling the vacancy left by the death of his close friend Rev. Theodore Wright.

Garnet's opinion that the conditions of blacks were deteriorating in America was confirmed by the Supreme Court ruling in March 1857 in the Dred Scott case. In effect, the court's dismissal of Scott's suit for freedom meant that the North could no longer be regarded as a completely safe sanctuary for blacks—fugitive or free. No longer were there areas where blacks could legally be protected.

Garnet reflected on a variety of strategies to meet this critical situation. He was certain that blacks must develop independent bases of political and economic power. His experiences both in separate movements in the 1840's and in Jamaica had taught him the value of black self-determination. Again he was prepared to seek a black nationalist solution to the problems of blacks. With repression of blacks increasing, he found that others were considering similar ideas.

The concept of group solidarity and nationality that had been implicit in the ideas of various black abolitionists for years was openly expressed in the 1850's. A new nationalist thinking was beginning to arise, and Garnet and others wanted to be in a position to stimulate its spread.

CHAPTER SIX

"A Grand Center of Negro Nationality"

National consciousness has always been present in the life of blacks. Deeply rooted in the black experience, the development of this consciousness can be traced to the arrival of the first slaves in America. In the South, slave rebellions and the maintenance of Africanisms were prominent features of black national consciousness. In the North it was expressed in the early nineteenth-century state and national Negro conventions, the formation of black churches, schools, and benevolent societies, the vigilance committees to aid fugitive slaves and to protect the black community from attack by racist whites. Black self-improvement societies in New York City and other Northern cities gave tremendous support to Joseph Cinque and the African rebels who seized the slaver *Amistad* and liberated themselves.

By 1850, many blacks had come to feel that they could not advance in America. They began to consider settling in other areas of the world. Emigration soon became the dominant goal of the new nationalists. Within this movement, a number of projects were considered. A few individuals felt that the time was opportune to channel emigrationist sentiment into a viable program.

In late 1853, a call for a national emigration convention went out. The call was signed by twenty-six blacks, including Martin Delany, William Webb, A. M. Sumner, and James M. Whitfield. The convention was scheduled for August 1854 in Cleveland. They were convinced that blacks could never achieve dignity and self-respect until they were in a position to control their own affairs. In short, they must be the "ruling element in the society in which [they] live."[1] The convention was an effort to give structure to an idea that Garnet and several others had earlier voiced.

In February 1849, Garnet had pointed to the possible benefits of emigration: "I am in favor of colonization in any part of the United States, Mexico or California, or in the West Indies, or Africa, wherever it promises freedom and enfranchisement. Other people became great and powerful by colonization."[2] Liberia, which gained its independence in 1847 and stood as the world's second black nation, seemed to Garnet to hold the most promise for the future. He outlined three reasons he felt Liberian development would strengthen the position of black people in America and the world:

1. I believe that the Republic of Liberia will be highly beneficial to Africa in a commercial and a political point.
2. I believe that the new Republic will succeed—and that its success will curtail the slave trade on the coast, by the diffusion of light and knowledge, and by turning the attention of the black traders to some other and honorable business, and by sweeping off the white ones as with the hands of an avenging God. . . .
3. I believe that every political and commercial relation which President Roberts negotiates with European powers goes far to create respect for our race throughout the civilized world. . . . It is my firm and sober belief, that Liberia will become the Empire State of Africa.[3]

If Liberia or any other country offered hope to blacks, then they should take it. Emigration, Garnet explained to Frederick Douglass, was "the source of wealth, prosperity and independence."[4] He buttressed his argument by citing the fact that the rich and propertied had unchecked control over the sources of power in America: "Those who dwell in the Eastern and Middle states will be crushed to death by old aristocratic arrangements, and by the ponderous wheels of wealth and the various forms of monopoly."[5]

In 1853, by the time of the convention, black public opinion had shifted dramatically in favor of emigration. Nearly every spokesman, though, was careful to disassociate the objectives of emigration from those of the hated American Colonization Society. The society sought to drain off free blacks to Liberia through deportation, thus leaving slavery intact. Colonizationists thought free blacks were a menace to the plantation economy, a disruptive element among the "tranquil" slave population. The American Colonization Society always enjoyed the solid support of a majority of the Southern planters.

The emigrationists emphasized that their movement was voluntary and selective. Their thinking represented a genuine strain of expression among blacks. It was not imposed on the black community by whites, like colonization. It sprang from a desire to promote black self-determination and control. Emigration was a legitimate reaction to an intolerably oppressive situation. The emigrationists contended that they supported the basic aims of the abolitionist struggle. Some even called for increasing arms for self-defense and slave rebellions. The thirty-one-point Declaration of Sentiments drawn up by the convention somewhat reflected this view:

19. That no oppressed people have ever obtained their rights by voluntary acts of generosity on the part of their oppressors.
20. That it is futile hope on our part to expect such

good results through the agency of moral good-
ness on the part of our white American oppressors.[6]

This theme also ran through several of the speeches.
H. Ford Douglass in the keynote address stated:

I can hate this Government without being disloyal
because it has stricken down my manhood, and
treated me as a saleable commodity. I can join a
foreign enemy and fight against it, without being a
traitor, because it treats me as an alien and a stranger,
and I am free to avow that should such a contingency
arise I should not hesitate to take any advantage in
order to procure indemnity for the future.[7]

Douglass summed up the feelings of the convention when
he related that "the expediency of a 'colored nationality,'
is becoming self-evident to Colored men more and more
every day." The Declaration of Sentiments also asserted
the need for race pride, unity, self-determination, the
obliteration of class distinctions among blacks, acquisition
of land, and economic development.

Black women were prominent in convention activities.
One was a vice-president, and four others sat on the finance
committee. The convention represented the most advanced
thinking of the times. It focused on building a militant
mass movment. No one advocated a wholesale black
exodus from the country.

Critics such as Frederick Douglass, Nell, and J. M. Langston equated the ideas of the convention's sponsors with
those of the white colonizationists. They believed the convention sidetracked energies from the black liberation
struggle in America.

Earlier, Garnet had met with similar criticism when he
complimented colonizationists who were sincerely contributing to the growth of Africa. He had written that he
"would rather see a man free in Liberia, than a slave in

the United States."[8] For this, Ward had accused him of aligning with the colonizationists. In reply, Garnet emphatically stated that he had "experienced no change of mind as to the possibility of our enfranchisement in this land of our birth."[9] He added that he was still firmly against the schemes of the American Colonization Society.

As long as Garnet alone had articulated his ideas, there was no loud outcry. When the movement became organized, response was different. Douglass used the full weight of his paper to denounce the convention's sponsors. Others followed suit. Whitfield, who would later attempt to lead an exploratory mission to Central America, rebutted emigration opponents with the rejoinder that the oppressed must be allowed to "work out their own salvation."[10]

In the debate that ensued nearly every black leader lined up on one side or the other. It was clear that neither side really understood the position of the other. The emigrationists appeared to see in black opposition to their aims a desire to remain under the dictates of whites. This was not the case. Douglass by this time had moved far from his earlier position as a Garrisonian. The 1853 national Negro convention, of which he and Langston were sponsors, passed resolutions nearly identical in substance to those adopted at the emigration convention. The 1853 convention set up at Douglass' insistence a National Council of the Colored People to develop economic and political power among blacks.

The anti-emigrationists were off-base in their charges that the sponsors of the emigration convention had abandoned the struggle. The resolutions passed by the emigrationists proved that their dedication to liberation had not lessened. In fact, it was stronger than ever. The convention recognized that blacks could never be free anywhere until slavery was destroyed in America.

This conviction was solidly held by Martin Delany, whose writings laid the theoretical foundations for the new nationalism of the emigrationists. In the *Mystery*, a newspaper he published in the 1840's, Delany had staunchly supported the principles of group action and black economic independence. In 1853, in a letter opposing the establishment by Harriet Beecher Stowe of an industrial school for blacks, he declared: "no enterprise, institution, or anything else, should be commenced for us, or our general benefit, without first consulting us."[11] In his major work, *The Condition, Elevation, Emigration and Destiny of the Colored People of the United States,* Delany analyzed the main issues of concern to blacks. These included classes, the control of wealth, racism, religion, education, Africa, and world history. He emphasized the necessity for blacks to run their own organizations and determine their own affairs:

> Our elevation must be the result of *self-effort,* and work of our *own hands.* No other human power can accomplish it. If we but determine it shall be so, it will be so. Let each one make the case his own, and endeavor to rival his neighbor, in honorable competition.[12]

Stress on emigration was only one facet of the new black nationalism. A few blacks examined the positive dimensions of black history. To them it was a source of pride and a means of combating the racist myths about blacks in Africa and America perpetuated by whites. Garnet must be included among this group of pioneer black historians.* In

* Even before 1850, black lecturers commonly referred to the glory and achievements of Africa. David Nickens in an address in 1832 noted that "all the now civilized world is indebted to Africa for the arts of civilization." Published works by blacks on this subject included Pennington's *Text Book of the Origin and History of the Colored People* (1841) and R. B. Lewis' *Light and Truth: Collected from the Bible and Ancient and Modern History, Containing the Universal History of the Colored and Indian Race* (1844). After 1850, there were Ward's "Origin, History and Hopes of the Negro Race" (1850), William G. Allen's "The Origin and History of the Africans" (1850), and Douglass' "The Claims of the Negro Ethnologically Considered" (1854). Others, like Beman

an address before the Female Benevolent Society in Troy in February 1848, he dealt at length with the history of ancient Africa.† He placed the blame for the destruction of African institutions on Western society:

> By an almost common consent, the modern world seems determined to pilfer Africa of her glory. It were not enough that her children have been scattered over the globe, clothed in the garments of shame—humiliated and oppressed—but her merciless foes weary themselves in plundering the tombs of our renowned sires, and in obliterating their worthy deeds, which were inscribed by fame upon the pages of ancient history.[13]

He went on to describe the Ethiopians and Egyptians as blacks who had originated science and learning. Africa had produced an enlightened and orderly society while the Europeans were still groping in ignorance and superstition:

> At this time, when these representatives of our race were filling the world with amazement, the ancestors of the now proud and boasting Anglo Saxons were among the most degraded of the human family. They abode in caves under ground, either naked or covered with the skins of wild beasts.[14]

He predicted that Africa would once again emerge as a modern and thriving continent, ranking as a world power.
  Garnet made his customary references to slave rebels

and Jeremiah B. Sanderson, prepared formal lectures on the history of Africa and the black world. In 1855, Nell published his, *The Colored Patriots of the American Revolution,* which was the first real source book on Afro-American history. Later, during the 1860's and 1870's, Brown followed with similar texts, entitled *The Black Man, The Rising Son,* and *The Negro in the American Rebellion.* Delany contributed an essay, "The International Policy of the World Towards the African Race" (1867).
  † The complete text of this speech is in Appendix Seven.

in Haiti, Cuba, and America, whose heroism had shaken the very foundations of oppression. He had nothing but praise for the blacks of Haiti for their efforts to build an independent nation. He used the occasion to criticize blacks who seemed concerned more with wealth and personal possessions than with the struggle for freedom. He was completely aware that blacks were not united in their commitment to the anti-slavery movement.

In the North, a tiny black elite had arisen. Its members were businessmen and tradesmen in barbering, catering, contracting, and other occupations. There were also a few skilled black professionals who were employed as teachers, lawyers, and doctors. It has been estimated that by the Civil War this group had accumulated $50 million in real and personal wealth.

In the South, particularly in Louisiana and Virginia, a few free blacks owned plantations with a large supply of slaves for labor. Carter G. Woodson, who from the census of 1830 compiled statistics on the number of slaves held by black planters, concluded that some blacks did purchase slaves for purposes of economic gain rather than for humanitarian reasons.[15]

A small number of free blacks, in both North and South, maintained a stake in the perpetuation of the system.* According to E. Franklin Frazier:

> The savings and business undertakings on the part of the free Negroes reflected the spirit and values of their environment. Through thrift and saving, white American artisans hoped to accumulate wealth and get ahead. This spirit was encouraged among the free Negroes by their leaders.[16]

Garnet felt that the fight should be for total liberation and should not be over trivialities such as names and

* Several black leaders were concerned about this problem. Walker in his *Appeal* and Ward in his *Autobiography* scored the black elite for their indifference. Frances Watkins also took them to task in the *Anglo-African Magazine* (May 1859).

labels. Whether blacks were called "Negroes" or "Afric-Americans" did not matter if they were still slaves. The paramount issue was survival. All attempts to spread slavery had to be stopped. Garnet condemned the government for perpetrating the Mexican War:

> The genius of slavery in this country has taken its course southward. . . . It has laid its hands upon the nation's standard, and has urged its way through flood, and field, until that blood-stained banner waves on the halls of the Montezumas. It claims its victories on the ensanguined plains of Monterey, Cerro Gordo, Chapultepec, Churubusco, and Buena Vista, and hangs out its stiffened and gory garments from the old grey walls of Vera Cruz.[17]

In Jamaica, Garnet had realized that the conditions of blacks there were in some ways similar to those of blacks in the United States. This being the case, perhaps, he thought, emphasis on struggle in America alone was too narrow. Maybe a broadly based international movement to promote unity within the entire black world, from Africa to the Caribbean, should be organized.

During the summer of 1858, Garnet and several other blacks and interested whites founded the African Civilization Society. He was elected the society's first president. The goals and structure of the group were formulated in twelve articles. Membership in the society was open to all. The officers, elected by the general body, were required to hold office for a year. Decisions about governing the group were in the hands of a twenty-member board of directors, of which the president, vice-presidents, secretaries, and treasurer were ex officio members.

The founders insisted that the society had not been formed to support the colonization society, but the suspicions of some black leaders were not allayed. They pointed out that Ben Coates, a Quaker merchant from Philadelphia who had for years been identified with the colonizationists, was a ranking officer of the society. This seemed to indicate a connection between the two organizations.

There was perhaps a slight element of truth in the charges of these leaders. Coates and a few other white backers probably saw an opportunity to push their colonizationist ideas through the society with the cooperation of respected blacks. In a letter to R. R. Gurley, secretary of the American Colonization Society, Coates said as much: "Many consider the African Civilization Society only African colonization under another name which it really is, except that it professes to be anti-slavery."[18] Some speculated that the new group hoped to attract blacks who might lean toward the colonization society's program for repatriation.

The society's saving grace with these critics was the presence of Garnet and Joshua Giddings, both of whom were recognized for their work in the abolitionist movement. Over the years each had waged a vigorous fight against the colonizationists' scheme. Also, one of the articles of the society forbade dispatching to Africa any agents, missionaries, or settlers who sympathized with "doctrines which shall justify or aid in perpetuating any system of slavery or involuntary servitude."[19] It specified too that the society would work only with other societies that were in complete accord with the program of the African Civilization Society.

The society viewed the establishment of political and economic ties with Africa as a key to the destruction of the slave trade. It held that this could be accomplished by

> the introduction of lawful commerce and trade into Africa: the promotion of the growth of cotton and other products there, whereby the natives may become industrious producers as well as consumers of articles of commerce: and generally, the elevation of the condition of the colored population of our country, and of other lands.[20]

The plan to develop cotton as a staple crop within the economy of Africa was not novel. The British had undertaken a similar project earlier in areas of East Africa, and a few commercial investors in America had considered doing this. A white minister, T. J. Bowen, who had written a favorable account of West African society in his book *Central Africa,* published in 1857, suggested that the United States government establish relations with the Yoruba kings. He thought the Yorubas were a potential market for American goods and a possible source of agricultural products.

A few black abolitionists considered the disruptive effects that growing cotton and other crops in Africa for use in the world market would have on the economy of the South. William Whipper, in an article in *Douglass' Monthly* in March 1859, argued that this approach could benefit the anti-slavery movement.

Coates put the matter most clearly. Though not necessarily concerned with slavery in America, he proposed in his pamphlet *The Cultivation of Cotton in Africa* the organization "of emigrant aid societies in each state to form settlements in Yoruba, Soudan and other portions of the high table land of Central Africa."

Garnet enthusiastically embraced this idea. He agreed that the base of slavery could be weakened through the wider use of free labor and the building of an alternative African supply of cotton. He was undoubtedly influenced by the second and third national emigration conventions, held in 1856 and 1858. At the latter convention, in Chatham, Ontario, Delany had laid final plans for his Niger Valley expedition.* In an earlier proposal for this

* The establishment of black settlements in Africa was an old idea. In 1795 the Free African Society of Newport, Rhode Island, sent a member to Sierra Leone to explore sites. Later Paul Cuffe, through black-led societies and his own organization, the Friendly Society of Sierra Leone, transported a group of black emigrants to West Africa in 1816. In 1850, the Cincinnati Emigration Association recommended that agents be sent to Africa to purchase land "to

expedition, Delany had examined East Africa's potential for economic development:

> it presents the greatest facilities for an immense trade, with China, Japan, Siam, Hindoostan, in short, all the East Indies—of any other country in the world. With a settlement of enlightened freemen, who with the immense facilities, must soon grow into a powerful nation.[21]

Delany believed his expedition had tremendous implications for the black struggle in America.

Though aware of the African Civilization Society, Delany was not interested in actually joining it. He felt that there was too much white influence on the members. He also was not completely certain about Garnet, who in the past had solicited money from wealthy white abolitionists. In personal letters to Gerrit Smith, Garnet had asked for funds to carry on programs. Although Delany never questioned Garnet's integrity, he thought that this policy was detrimental to the forming of a black organization and that support should always come entirely from the blacks themselves.

Delany's position on this issue was basically sound. The control and decisions of a group usually flowed from its financial backers. Often, white abolitionists would under-

---

establish a nationality." In addition, individual blacks had been emigrating to Africa since 1800. The most prominent were Dan Coker, a founder of the A.M.E. Church, who settled in Sierra Leone; Lott Cary, a well-known clergyman; and John Russwurm, publisher of *Freedom's Journal,* who settled in Liberia. Several blacks also published accounts of their trips to West Africa: Cuffe's *A Brief Account of the Settlement and Present Situation of the Colony of Sierra Leone in Africa* (1812), Daniel H. Peterson's *The Looking Glass: Being a True Report and Narrative of the Rev. Daniel H. Peterson a Colored Clergyman: Embracing a Period of Time from the Year 1812 to 1854 and Including His Visit to Western Africa* (1854), and Samuel Williams' *Four Years in Liberia* (1857).

write a black organization. Invariably the organization would be stripped not only of its militancy but also of its responsiveness to the immediate needs of the black community.

Delany had formed an all-black National Board of Commissioners, which would be responsible for working out details of the Niger Valley expedition. The board would ensure that control of the finances would be by blacks for blacks.

Throughout the last part of 1858, Garnet traveled extensively, lecturing on both the anti-slavery movement and the program of the African Civilization Society. By the summer of 1859, he was devoting most of his efforts to promoting African development. In August, he wrote that the founding of a powerful African nation "would do more for the overthrowing of slavery, in creating a respect for ourselves, than fifty thousand lectures of the most eloquent men of this land."[22]

In May 1859, Delany had sailed for Africa. Toward the end of preparing for his trip, he had changed his plans. He would explore the area of the upper Niger, rather than go farther south as he had originally intended. Delany's change of plan was probably influenced by the African Civilization Society; the upper Niger was the territory it had chosen to explore.[23] Two of the members of the planned five-man expedition party dropped out before Delany sailed. Robert Campbell, a Jamaica-born instructor at the Colored Institute in Philadelphia, laid out the prospectus of the trip. The three main goals were to select a location for an industrial colony, promote enterprise, and weaken slavery through cotton production.[24]

Campbell, after receiving funds from the Civilization Society at Garnet's request, sailed for Africa in June 1859. In Africa, he reunited with Delany. In December 1859, they signed a treaty with eight kings of the Abbeokuta. The treaty's four articles provided for Afro-American settlement on any unused land, respect for the laws and customs of the Egba people, possession of skills by the settlers, and self-government. The treaty was clearly within the aims of the expedition. In the official report, Delany wrote:

> Our policy must be—and I hazard nothing in promulgating it; nay, without this design and feeling, there would be a great deficiency of self-respect, pride of race, and love of country, and we might never expect to challenge the respect of nations—*Africa for the African race, and black men to rule them.*[25]

After the signing, Campbell immediately addressed a letter to Garnet announcing the treaty. Garnet then called a meeting of the African Civilization Society to secure support for the idea of settlement in Abbeokuta. He wanted to take advantage of what he saw as the first link in solidifying relations between Africa and Afro-America. He assured Campbell, "We have now a number of men who are willing to embark on this glorious enterprise and who believe as I do—that there is a glorious future for Africa."[26] He did not go into detail about where the money and material would come from or how the people would be selected for the settlement. The only person who seemed certain about their plans was Campbell, who in the journal (later published as *A Pilgrimage to My Motherland*) he kept of the trip stated that he intended to live in Africa.

Delany was also impressed by Africa. He wrote to Garnet, describing Lagos as potentially "a great commercial city" and "entirely under a black government."[27]

The actions of Delany, Campbell, and Garnet must be regarded as significant feats of the early black nationalist movement. They pushed the movement beyond rhetoric. Through their own efforts, black men had established ties with an African people. In doing so, they had placed themselves in the position of sovereign nations. The treaty was a tangible symbol of the bond of mutual respect and recognition extended from both sides. The African kings and the members of the Niger Valley exploring party accepted each other as brothers and as men. This could not help but give pride and dignity to oppressed blacks in America. Even those, like Douglass, who took a dim view of the whole affair were forced to admit this.

The nationalist movement continued to grow during 1859. One element that the movement lacked was a theoretical organ. In 1859 this was partly remedied with the founding of the *Anglo-African Magazine* and the *Weekly Anglo-African* newspaper by Robert and Thomas Hamilton. The two brothers were black printers in New York City. Although the Hamiltons were not committed to the goals of the emigrationists, they intended their publications to reflect the views of all segments of the black population. In the magazine's first editorial, Thomas Hamilton explained: "In addition to an exposé of the condition of the blacks, this Magazine will have the aim to uphold and encourage the now depressed hopes of thinking black men, in the United States."[28]

The newspaper diligently reported the speeches and statements of the proponents of African and West Indian development. Controlled by blacks, the Hamiltons' publications took a strong nationalist position on various issues. Garnet, Delany, Douglass, Nell, and Frances Watkins were listed as contributing editors to the *Weekly Anglo-African*. The paper, in its September 10, 1859, issue, carried the complete proceedings of a meeting held by blacks in Boston, where Garnet had delivered a lecture on the African Civilization Society. The meeting, chaired by J. Sella Martin, a young minister and Garnet protégé, had been called in order to provide Garnet with a forum for answering the critics of the society.

In his introductory remarks, Martin attacked black leaders in Boston who had refused to lend their facilities to Garnet for a society meeting. He also criticized the New

England Colored Citizens Convention, held several weeks earlier, for its failure to support the goals of the African Civilization Society.

Garnet and his group believed that the convention had been called just to attack the society. George Downing, the convention's president, along with Nell and Brown, had repeatedly denounced the society. Their attitude seemed paradoxical because the convention had been willing to go on record with a resolution praising the progress of the Haitians as a confirmation of black "capacity for self-government."[29]

Garnet began his speech by accusing the New England Colored Citizens Convention of not being a true black gathering. The convention had been managed by self-seeking whites. Garnet was especially incensed because the convention had totally "misrepresented his views on the African Civilization Society" and "on the great subject of humanity." Garnet clashed with Nell, who was present, over the convention sponsors' motives for attacking him. Nell denied that there had been a preconceived plan to vilify Garnet. So there would be no misunderstanding, Garnet sought to clarity his position. What he wanted to establish was a "grand center of negro nationality, from which shall flow the streams of commercial, intellectual and political power which shall make colored people respected everywhere."[30] He could not see how his advocacy of this made him a colonizationist. In fact, he bluntly characterized as "liars" those who labeled him as one.

No sooner had Garnet finished than there were objections from the floor. One questioner asked whether this "negro nationality" was to be built in Africa or in America. Garnet responded:

I hope in the United States; especially if they reopen the African slave trade. Then, if we do not establish a nationality in the South, I am mistaken in the spirit of my people. Let them bring in a hundred thousand a year! We do not say it is not a great crime, but we

know that from the wickedness of man God brings
forth good; and if they do it, before half a century
shall pass over us we shall have a negro nationality
in the United States. In Jamaica there are forty
colored men to one white; Haiti is ours; Cuba will be
ours soon, and we shall have every island in the
Caribbean Sea.[31]

This is a clear and prophetic statement of the Pan-
African ideal. Curiously, Garnet stressed the South as the
section where black self-determination would be realized.
He anticipated the movement for local control, from Reconstruction on, that would focus on the black-belt area
of the South.

At the close of the meeting, Martin offered a series of
resolutions commending Garnet for his work in the struggle. He was careful to exclude any mention of the African
Civilization Society and emigration. Apparently feeling
that the audience was too divided on these issues, he pre-
ferred not to attempt to gain endorsement for the society's
program. The resolutions, which were broad enough to be
agreed on by all, were quickly passed.

In the following months, the attacks against Garnet
increased. The bitterest opponents of the new nationalism
continued to be black leaders who at one time had been
aligned with the Garrisonians. Douglass in particular remained strongly against Garnet and the African Civilization Society. In reply to a rebuke by Garnet, Douglass outlined seven major criticisms of the organization's program:
(1) America is the black man's home; (2) the struggle for
the abolition of slavery should be fought in America, not
Africa; (3) (4) this applies to the fight against the slave
trade as well; (5) the most effective organization against
slavery must be where slavery actually is—in America, not
in Africa; (6) producing cotton in Africa to depress Southern prices is impracticable; (7) the civilization society,
whether intentionally or not, is doing the same work as the
colonization society.[32] Douglass did defend the right of

individuals to emigrate if they felt that they could better their status by doing so.

This criticism did not settle the issue in Douglass' mind. In another editorial, he sided with those who had opposed Garnet at the Boston meeting. He chided Garnet for answering the objectors rather than dealing with their objections. He further contended:

> We are perfectly willing, of course, and it is ridiculous to pretend that we are not, that enterprising colored men, self-moved, and self-sustained should go either to Africa or Australia, or anywhere else, to promote their individual fortune. But it is quite a different thing when we are asked to join such men and assist them in their private enterprises.[33]

Douglass' Monthly concluded by accusing Garnet of begging whites for money for a project supposedly in the interests of blacks.

Douglass' point about the desirability of emigration in any form was certainly well taken. Despite the fact that emigration grew out of desire for national development, the black community as a whole had not had an adequate opportunity to express its feelings about the ramifications of such a move. The emigration movement was vulnerable to opportunists.

The overriding question was never asked. Would the masses of blacks have genuine control over the mechanisms of power in the proposed black settlement or nation? Would emigration serve their interests or the interests of the black elite? The blacks who had already emigrated to Liberia had proven to be so thoroughly Americanized that they had actually tried to subjugate the indigenous tribal groupings in a manner similar to that used by foreign colonialists: "Unfortunately those in control took their cue for the treatment of the natives from the slaveholders of the United States by whom their forebears were . . . sent to Africa."[34] This was not the way to build a black nation, let alone effect black liberation.

Douglass' criticism that Garnet was "begging" whites for money was not accurate. Although Garnet did solicit funds from Smith, he was opposed on principle to black organizations' accepting white money. In his speech at the Boston meeting, he said it was time for black groups to become truly independent and control their own finances. It was no longer tolerable for blacks to be borrowers; they must strive instead to be lenders. Black professionals should be encouraged and supported in order to build pride and respect and a firm economic base for the community.

The charge of begging was also leveled against Garnet by Brown in an article in the October 22, 1859, issue of the *Weekly Anglo-African*. Taking it a step further, Brown labeled the entire African Civilization Society a "begging concern" and offered to contribute fifty dollars toward sending Garnet to Africa on the condition that he not return to America for five years.

Although Brown's article showed the ridiculous depths to which the debate had sunk, it did indicate the bitterness the issue had engendered. Neither faction was willing to compromise. The division in the ranks of the liberationists hurt the anti-slavery cause. The leaders involved in the debate had known each other for years and had shared experiences in the abolitionist movement. Exactly which segment of the black community these leaders purported to speak for was often unclear. The masses had little opportunity to voice their opinions on these questions. While the leaders debated the fine points, most Northern blacks were concerned over just how emigration or integration related practically to their most immediate needs. Because Douglass, Garnet, and the others failed to realize this, the masses were the losers. The controversy was a dispute between personalities rather than over ideas.

Garnet used every meeting and rally he spoke at during the early part of 1860 to push the issue of African reconstruction. In March, in a speech at Cooper's Institute in New York City, he detailed the principal objectives of the African Civilization Society.* At no time, he remarked, had the society attempted to discourage blacks from struggling in America: "We reject the idea, entertained by many, that the black man can never enjoy equal privileges in this country with other classes."[35] Garnet was followed by other speakers, black and white, who affirmed the society's aim to work for the destruction of slavery. A local black minister, Dr. Asa Hague, perhaps best summed up the society's perspective on this matter:

> It was a popular idea that prejudice against color was connected with the idea of slavery. Nothing could be more incorrect, for in the sixth century, in the time of Justinian, slaves were white. In order to subdue this prejudice and to elevate the race, there must be a nationalization; and in order to bring the community together, scattered as it is far and wide, one grand center must exist. The people must have a nation, a commerce, a system of diplomacy.[36]

The speeches did not silence the critics. Garnet proposed to debate with Rev. James N. Gloucester, who had been especially vocal in his attacks on the society. A public meeting was scheduled at the Zion Church in New York City for April 12, 1860. The announcement for the meeting, put out by the society's opponents, equated the group with the old colonization scheme. They labeled the society "a supporter of prejudice."[37] Eighteen well-known black community leaders signed this announcement. Totally distorting the society's aims, they declared:

COLORED MEN READ

It is said we should be slaves. It is said we should go to Africa. A new society has been formed to send us there. It is collecting money for that purpose. Shall

* Part of this speech is in Appendix Eight.

this be? Will you be shipped off? A public meeting to oppose the same is to be held. . . . Let nothing prevent you: come out, come out; crowd old Zion.[38]

Clearly these men intended to pull out all the stops in their campaign against Garnet and the African Civilization Society. They had even enlisted the aid of prominent figures such as Gerrit Smith, Purvis, Nell, Brown, and Garrison. These individuals had been asked to send letters to the meeting denouncing the society.

The audience, predominantly black, was composed almost equally of supporters and opponents of the society. Downing, who opened the meeting, suggested that each speaker confine his remarks to fifteen minutes. Debate immediately broke out over the selection of officers. Each side maneuvered to have its backers run the meeting. After a brief jostling, Garnet and Martin grudgingly accepted the officers chosen by Downing, with the understanding that the meeting be open to all views.

What followed was a series of sharp exchanges between Garnet and Downing, primarily over how the meeting was to be conducted. After this, Downing offered ten resolutions condemning the African Civilization Society for employing agents in Europe, misrepresenting the black cause, being an appendage of the American Colonization Society, and creating divisions within the anti-slavery movement. The final resolution stated:

Resolved, That our hope for the emancipation of the slave in this country does not rest either on the cultivation of cotton in Africa, nor on the building up of a negro nationality there; but on the radical change of public opinion here, to be brought about by a continued anti-slavery agitation.[39]

A general uproar began when Downing finished and moved for the adoption of the resolutions. Garnet, taking advantage of the chaotic situation, demanded that the resolutions be thrown out. In the confusion no one challenged him, so he declared his motion carried and asked the audience to go home.

Garnet, however, knew that the matter was not closed. Stung by the criticism, he attempted to dispel the idea that there was any semblance of a connection between his organization and the colonizationists'. Several days later, at a meeting of the society, he personally raised a motion opposing the American Colonization Society. He emphasized again that the African Civilization Society's main purpose was to destroy slavery. In a speech, he called upon blacks to aid Africa and Haiti in their efforts to develop a labor force both "systematic and productive" as a means of countering slavery.[40]

The society's opponents had no intention of dropping the fight. In an article in the *Weekly Anglo-African,* James McCune Smith, his old friend and rival, claimed that Garnet's support of the Niger Valley expedition party had been an acceptance of slavery. He contended that the Abbeokuta kings practiced slavery within their society, and he urged Garnet to wash his "hands of a treaty which commits your association to respect the institution of domestic slavery."[41]

In the next edition of the paper, Garnet called Smith's allegations totally unfounded. The society, he maintained, took no part in any of the plans made by Delany's group. The expedition had been a completely independent venture:

> These enterprising, learned, and intelligent gentlemen, never were for a single period known in the time table—are not now, and probably never will be commissioners of the African Civilization Society. They went out and returned, and published their papers and books as "Commissioners of the Niger Valley Exploring Party."[42]

Smith's accusations that he condoned slavery were too ridiculous for words. He could not understand how anyone who knew of his lifelong work in the abolitionist movement could utter such a charge. Garnet considered this a direct slap at his integrity. He countered by asking Smith what he and others like him had contributed to the black liberation struggle. He reminded Smith that he and other well-to-do blacks had consistently refused to support the establishment of a reading room for black youth in New York City or to patronize black tradesmen:

> And you anti-emigrationists, Dr. Smith, are no better in this respect than your hard-hearted white brethren. You likewise "do not employ niggers." You pass by the black tailor, mantus-maker, milliner, and shocmaker and carpenter, and employ white people who curse you to your teeth. Why your own party will not even employ a black doctor as a general thing. A few weeks ago an Irish gentleman showed me a beautiful mansion on the thriving Sixth Avenue, which to your great credit belongs to you. I looked upon it, and felt proud of the success of my early friend. As I saw the stately pile, and heard the merry music of the trowel, hammer, and plane, I looked in vain to discover a dark face at work. There was not one there—no, not even a hod carrier. By the side of your property, another equally imposing structure was going up, owned by the Rev. James N. Gloucester, and I saw there also an entire absence of the practical application of your professed principles. . . . Tell me, do you even go so far as to hire your houses to black people? There is one colored tradesman whom you patronize, that is the black "barber," for no one else will shave you.[43]

Garnet's plans received a boost from two prominent blacks who had emigrated to Africa. Crummell had left America in 1847 and traveled to England, where he received a degree from Cambridge University. From there, he had gone to Liberia as a missionary and worked tirelessly for Liberian national development. In September 1860, Crummell addressed an open letter on "The Relations and Duties of the Free Colored Men in America to Africa." In it he appealed to blacks:

> to give, even of your best, to save, and regenerate, and build up the *race* in distant quarters. You should study to rise above the niggard spirit which grudgingly and pettishly yields its grasp upon a fellow laborer. You should claim in regard to this continent that *"This is our Africa."*[44]

Crummell believed in and fully supported the program of the African Civilization Society. In the same letter, he stated that the society "sets forth my views in better language than my own."

Edward Wilmot Blyden, the West Indian–born educator, was another strong backer of African reconstruction. Blyden, who settled in Liberia in 1851, had rapidly ascended to a position of prominence in governmental affairs there. In the late 1850's, he and Crummell tried to interest Afro-Americans in their plans for a black university in Liberia that would serve as a Pan-African "center of learning."

Blyden traveled extensively outside of Africa in an effort to promote a favorable impression of Liberia. Like Garnet, he contended that the growth of Liberia into a strong and independent black nation would gain both international respect for blacks and weaken the slave trade. In his pamphlet *A Voice from Bleeding Africa,* published in 1856, he wrote:

> it is the earnest desire of Liberians to see American slavery speedily abolished. They are determined to give countenance to no act that, in their opinion, tends either directly or indirectly to strengthen that nefarious system; but will gladly avail themselves of every expedient that they consider, in any way, ac-

celerative of the enfranchisement of the millions of
their brethren on the other side of the Atlantic. Their
object is, the redemption of Africa and the disenthral-
ment and elevation of the African race.*

Blyden and Crummell were ecstatic over the Niger Valley expedition. When Delany arrived in Liberia, Blyden was
chiefly responsible for arranging public meetings for him
in Monrovia, the capital. At one such meeting, Delany
received sustained applause when he said, "the desire for
African nationality has brought me to these shores."[45]
Garnet was also pleased over the emergence of a small
band of native African intellectuals who had begun to contribute their talents to the cause. One of these men, Dr.
James Horton, a physician and resident of Sierra Leone,
published two works in the 1860's: *The Political Economy
of British Western Africa, with the Requirements of the
Several Colonies and Settlements* (*The African View of the
Negro's Place in Nature*), and *West African Countries and
Peoples British and Native . . . and a Vindication of the
African Race.* In them Horton argued for political self-gov-
ernment for the various West African groups. He saw the
Fantee Confederation, along the coast of present-day
Ghana, as a meaningful model for local black control: "The
Fantee Confederation . . . and its main object is to advance
the interests of the whole of the Fantee nation, and to com-
bine for offence and defence in time of war."[46]

The popularity of the African Civilization Society increased. At a special meeting in November 1861 Delany
presented the findings of his trip to the members of the
society. All agreed that his objectives conformed with those
of their organization. After Delany's speech, a resolution

* Blyden insisted that Liberians were deeply concerned over the
progress of the black struggle in America. He related that Stephen
A. Benson, Liberia's second president, had an autographed por-
trait of Garnet on his wall with the signed inscription, "Better die
free men than live to be slaves."

was passed inviting him to join a special committee that would submit a report to the general committee of the society on the emigration movement. Following the meeting, Delany, Robert Hamilton, and a large group of black ministers became official members of the society. On their recommendation three articles were added to the society's constitution:

Article I

The Society is not designed to encourage general emigration, but will aid only such persons as may be practically qualified and suited to promote the development of Christianity, morality, education, mechanical arts, agriculture, commerce, and general improvement; who must always be carefully selected and well-recommended, that the progress of civilization may not be obstructed.

Article II

The basis of the Society, and ulterior objects in encouraging emigration, shall be—Self-Reliance and Self-Government, on the principle of an African Nationality, the African race being the ruling element of the nation, controlling and directing their own affairs.

Article III

All agents employed by this society must act under instructions, and consistently with the fundamental principles of the construction.

Clearly, these men brought to the society a sense of direction and perspective. With Garnet's support, Delany was installed as a vice-president. They hoped that these changes would turn the society into a genuine black organization.

His confidence bolstered by these new occurrences, Garnet began planning an expedition of his own to the Niger Valley. This idea was not new with him. He had earlier presented this plan to a meeting of the Friends of African Civilization in March 1861. Garnet intended to lead a select group to Africa. His goals were similar to Delany's. He estimated that the trip would require $10,000 and hoped to raise the funds primarily in the black community. At a subsequent meeting he received official sanction from the society for the trip. Rev. J. P. Thompson lauded Garnet for his work in the society. Thompson reiterated the society's aim to cultivate cotton in Africa as a means of ending slavery. He suggested that the South would have been in no position to secede if the plan of the society had been followed. Thompson saw a connection between Garnet's plans for a trip and the pursuit of the organization's goal. Garnet's idea, however, was never carried out. Apparently, reflecting on the time, effort, and resources needed for such an expedition, he decided to lay aside his plans. A greater consideration was probably the Civil War.

Blacks' support of the society was only temporary. With the advent of the war, the society experienced a sharp decline. Most of its backers threw themselves into the Northern war effort.

The society accomplished little of its stated program. It never succeeded in attracting the allegiance of the black masses; its supporters were a select group of the black community's religious and professional leaders. Although the society's program was an embryonic expression of Pan-African sentiment, it was markedly narrow in its analysis of existing African institutions. Garnet, Crummell, Blyden, and Delany tended to accept the prevailing racist notion that African people were in desperate need of Christianity and Western civilization. This idea was strongly held by most black ministers. Garnet stated: "We believe that Africa is to be redeemed by Christian civilization. . . . We hold it to be the duty of the Christians and philanthropists in America, either to send or carry the gospel and civilization into Africa."[47]

The society's intention to attack slavery was a positive aim. Its approach, however, left much to be desired. What seemed feasible on paper (the plan to develop African cotton) was certainly impracticable. It was unrealistic to think that a weak black merchant class could compete with the powers of Western Europe. In the middle of the nineteenth century the imperialist drive for colonial markets was beginning. Ronald Robinson and John Gallagher, in *Africa and the Victorians,* point out:

> Naval power was being used to break up the barriers of artificial monopoly and restriction whether European or African, so that trade could expand through the cracks, carrying with it the essentials of liberal civilisation and British paramountcy. To put trade into the hinterland of the Niger would increase British commerce. . . . By 1864 there were twenty-one British firms operating in the Delta and in points south, all ferociously competing against each other, bolstering the buying price of palm oil in Africa, even as its selling price was falling in Europe.[48]

To approach the British ruling class with a partnership proposal for financing an African expedition, as Delany and some members of the society had planned, was at best naïve and at worst opportunistic. Because of British pressure, the Abbeokuta kings later broke the treaty Delany had made with them. Attempting to join in exploitation would have proven disastrous to the black struggle in America as well as to the movement for political and economic independence in Liberia. This also could have made Garnet decide to cancel his trip.

Increasingly, Garnet began to feel that perhaps Africa was not the only place where an independent black nation could be established. He began to reconsider the possibilities Haiti offered. Unlike Africans, the Haitians had control of a national government and seemed amenable to the idea of having Afro-Americans emigrate to their country. In August 1859, the Haitian government, through its secretary of state, justice, and of worship, F. E. Du Bois, issued a "Call for Emigration" to American blacks. The government offered jobs, land, security, and respect to the emigrants. It also promised: "Every individual, the issue of African blood, may, immediately on arrival, declare his wish to be naturalized: and after one year's residence, he can become a citizen of Haiti, enjoying all his civil and political rights."[49] In the spirit of Pan-Africanism, Haiti was in effect extending citizenship unconditionally to the whole black world.

To expedite emigration, the government announced that it was opening offices and appointing agents in the United States. In November 1860, the Haitian Bureau was established in Boston, with James Redpath as general agent. The bureau issued a circular outlining the provisions for emigration. Haiti had anticipated the immediate settlement of one hundred thousand farmers and rural laborers. The government made it plain that it did not need traders, hairdressers, waiters, teachers, or clergymen. Redpath edited a booklet, *A Guide to Hayti,* to acquaint blacks with the country. The work contained descriptions of the land and official government documents on emigration.

Redpath considered Haiti the perfect place for black development: "In Hayti, a far different future is opened to the colored race. There, it can develop itself in freedom; there, exhibit its capacity and genius. Nowhere else is there such an opportunity presented."[50] Redpath discounted Liberia as being nothing but a colony run by whites.

There was no widespread opposition to the Haitian movement, as there had been to African emigration. A few blacks, however, did object to Redpath, a white man, being placed in charge of the bureau. Delany in particular felt that a movement to promote black interests should be led by blacks. Garnet, who in December 1860 had joined the staff of the bureau as resident agent for the city and state of New York, took sharp exception to Delany:

You are indignant at the acknowledgement of the leadership of a *white man* [Redpath] in any work that particularly concerns *black men.* . . . [Yet] I see by the newspapers that in the convention held in 1848 [*sic*] in Chatham, C. W., one *John Brown* was appointed leader—commander-in-chief—of the Harper's Ferry invasion. There were several black men there, able and brave; and yet John Brown was appointed leader. The unfortunate Stevens moved for the appointment and *one Dr. Martin R. Delany seconded the motion.* Now, sir, tell me where I shall find your consistency, as John Brown was a *very* white man—his face and glorious hairs were all white. I am done with you on that point, Dr. Delany. You ought to have accepted the office of surgeon under that great white leader, as a surgeon's place is in the rear, out of harm's way.[51]

Delany's objection to Redpath did not mean that he was against the goals of the Haitian movement. He stated: "Abstractly considered I have no objection to Haitian Emigration. Regarding it in the light of choosing one's own rulers, seeking self-government, aiding our self-emancipated brethren to sustain a Black Nationality . . . I agree with it."[52]

In Garnet's opinion the Haitian Bureau was the best apparatus for black emigration. As an agent, one of his first acts was to bless the ship *Janet Kidson,* which sailed from New York City in January 1861 carrying sixty-one black emigrants to Haiti. From January to April Garnet had scheduled a lecture tour of New York. He planned to talk about Haiti and its importance to American blacks.

In becoming involved with the Haitian movement, Garnet found himself on solid ground. By early 1861, Afro-Americans were more than ready to listen to the black nationalist leaders. They did not have the deep suspicions about Haiti that they had had about Liberia. Haiti had been born as a nation out of revolutionary struggle; Liberia was established as nothing more than an appendage of the racist American Colonization Society. Most blacks had a deep respect for the Haitians. It was not difficult to find ideologues for Haiti among American blacks.

During the 1850's several works had been written about black prospects in Haiti and the Caribbean. The oldest and most prominent publicist for Haiti was Rev. James Theodore Holly. In 1857, Holly, who had been negotiating with the Haitian government for several years concerning emigration, published a pamphlet, *A Vindication of the Capacity of the Negro Race for Self-Government.* He defended the Haitian revolution and urged blacks throughout the world to contribute to the country's growth. Later, in "Thoughts on Hayti," a series of articles in the *Anglo-African Magazine,* Holly said that it was the obligation of blacks to build strong nations:

> As to simple negro nationalities, we already have an abundance of them. Africa is full of them. . . . It will be seen that whether the field of our activity be directed to Hayti or Africa, the question narrows itself down to the work of removing the disabilities of existing negro nationalities.[53]

Holly received encouragement for his ideas from prominent blacks such as A. V. Thompson, Whitfield, Delany, and J. Dennis Harris. Harris, after an investment survey of Haiti, concluded that blacks could construct an "empire" in the Caribbean that would gain "the admiration of the world."[54] At the same time, Ward, who had emigrated to Jamaica, was promoting that country as the garden spot for the black nation.

Garnet viewed these developments as a positive trend. For a short period, he threw his efforts into strengthening the operations of the Haitian Bureau. He looked with delight when old-line opponents of emigration, Brown, Nell, and William J. Watkins, became agents for the bureau and Douglass actively promoted the bureau in his publication.

The flurry of enthusiasm for Haiti was also to be short-lived. With the Civil War rapidly escalating, Garnet resigned from the bureau and prepared to leave for England to get support for the North. In explaining his actions, the *Weekly Anglo-African*[55] quoted him as saying that the Liberian colonizationists were using the bureau for their own purposes and that he had "never advocated an emigration of labor but only of brain to Africa."* Whatever the reason, Garnet quickly perceived that Afro-Americans' stake in the outcome of the Civil War was gigantic.

When hostilities broke out, black nationalism, which in the 1850's had looked outward for a nation, in the 1860's was channeled into the mobilization for total war for black liberation in America.

---

* Garnet had not completely reversed himself on the subject of African reconstruction. In a speech delivered at a national Negro convention in 1864, he criticized those who could not see anything positive in the work of the African Civilization Society. He said his faith in the necessity for a "negro nationality" had not been shaken. A resolution offered on the society was hotly disputed by convention delegates. Garnet wanted a full endorsement. The old opponents, again led by Downing, wanted a condemnation. Finally, a compromise resolution was passed over Garnet's objection that "he would prefer no resolution rather than the one proposed."

CHAPTER SEVEN

Looking Ahead

Garnet did not confine his activities to the nationalist movement. In the first two years of his pastorship at Shiloh, he made numerous appearances before local abolitionist societies in New York. On one speaking tour through the western part of the state, he shared the platform with Douglass in several towns.

In New York City, he attempted to set up benevolence and aid programs for local blacks. After the first year, Garnet found that his church's treasury had been depleted. Unless money was obtained immediately, he would have to discontinue his community work. To sustain the programs, he figured that he needed a minimum of $250. Over the next few months, he addressed appeals to the black community and to his old abolitionist acquaintances. With the help of Gerrit Smith and the Tappans he was able to raise the money in a fairly short time. In appreciation, Garnet invited Smith to the city to lecture at his church.

In May 1858, Garnet attended the American Abolition Society's anniversary convention. In an address, he called for increased efforts to destroy slavery. As a member of the convention's executive committee, he took a leading role in formulating many of the resolutions.

After the convention, Garnet went to visit a number of towns in the Midwest. He spoke primarily to black audiences on the issue of the Fugitive Slave Act. While in Cincinnati, Garnet became embroiled in a controversy within the black community over the betrayal of two fugitive slaves. A "people's court" had been convened to try the traitor, a black man named Brodie. Garnet, who took part, displayed manacles and a bullwhip to show the brutality of the slave catchers. After almost no deliberation, Brodie was found guilty. As punishment, he received three hundred blows from a paddle (one for each dollar he had been paid) and was run out of the state.

The political ferment of the 1850's gradually spilled over into governmental affairs. The question of slavery provided the impetus for the formation of the Republican Party in 1856. The party, which grew out of the ranks of the short-lived Free Soil Party, attracted several prominent blacks.

Garnet, from the start, took a cautious approach toward the Republicans. His enthusiasm for the Free Soilers (he had attended their convention in 1848) did not lead him to endorse the Republicans. He did not fail to notice that although they had based their platform on opposition to the extension of slavery, they had not called for its complete abolition. The party sought to check the power of the Southern planters not through abolition but rather through compromise. Eric Foner points out that even though many former Liberty Party supporters joined the Republican Party in the 1850's, they still "disavowed the intention of attacking slavery in states where it already existed by direct federal action."[1]

As a consequence of this, Garnet wanted to see blacks support only those who had taken an uncompromising position against slavery as an institution. In September 1858, he was one of thirty-seven delegates present at the Colored Men's National Suffrage Convention in Troy. In a resolution, the convention advised "the eleven thousand colored voters of this State to concentrate their strength upon the Republican ticket for Governor &c, now before the people."[2]

Garnet led the opposition to this resolution. He pushed

instead for the convention to nominate the slate of candidates of the Radical Abolitionists. They were a small group mostly of old-line Liberty Party supporters who held no allegiance to either of the major political parties. They were independents whose prime concern was the total destruction of slavery. Garnet was supported by only five other delegates. Disappointed, he later wrote: "I could not have thought that colored men could have been so blind to their best interests."[3] To counter this, he proposed calling a state convention at Rochester to "redeem the honor of our people from the base and wicked committal of the miserable convention."[4] Garnet hoped that such a convention would endorse the Radical Abolitionists in the upcoming state elections. He planned a tour of New York to line up black support for the convention. He desired to have men such as Douglass and Loguen join him in his campaign. In the meantime, Garnet was doing all he could, as an individual, for the election of Gerrit Smith, who was running for governor on the Radical Abolitionist–sponsored People's State Ticket.

Most of the nationalists, like Garnet, advocated the violent overthrow of slavery. In May 1858, Martin Delany, William Webb, William C. Munroe, who was president of the Chatham Emigration Convention, and other Canadian blacks met with John Brown in order to draw up plans for a new provisional government in America. In secret proceedings, a forty-eight article "provisional constitution and ordinances for the people of the United States" was approved for the administration of the government. Officials were also elected. Osborne P. Anderson, a black printer, was chosen as one of two congressmen.

A plan was devised that called for the capturing of a government weapons arsenal and the establishment of a liberated corridor through the Alleghenies for escaping slaves. The planners hoped that this corridor would eventually become a free state. To augment their proposals, they intended to foment massive slave insurrections in the South.* Brown, in fact, personally appointed Mammy Pleasant, a black woman from San Francisco, as an agent to organize slaves for this purpose.[5]

Although Garnet did not participate in the Chatham meeting, he did know of Brown's moves. First introduced to Brown in 1848, Garnet had provided him with well-placed contacts among Northern blacks. Garnet, who had once called Brown "the only white man who really understands slavery," was largely responsible for his meeting Douglass. In February 1858, Brown had written Garnet in New York City, asking him to organize societies for the recruitment of blacks to his group. Impressed with Brown's sincerity, the following month he set up a meeting in Philadelphia with William Still, the underground railroad leader, Stephen Smith, a wealthy black businessman, and a few other selected persons. The meeting was held to enlist the financial assistance of local blacks for Brown.

Garnet became somewhat disillusioned with Brown when he was forced to cancel his plan of attack, which had been scheduled originally for the summer of 1858. When Brown did finally launch his venture against Harpers Ferry in October 1859, Garnet and other well-known blacks such as Tubman, Douglass, and Loguen, who had previously committed themselves to him, failed to participate. Of the black men who had met with Brown at Chatham, only Anderson took part in the action. There was some significance to the fact that, despite the obstacles,

* Delany had anticipated such an action. In his novel *Blake*, parts of which were written before he had knowledge of Brown and his ideas, Delany had prophesied successful slave rebellions in the South and Cuba. In one section, he borrows Garnet's motto for a dialogue between Henry, his main character, and another slave:

"An has yeh done it, Henry?" earnestly inquired Andy.
"Yes, Andy; yes, I have done it! and I thank God for it! I have taught the slave that mighty lesson: to strike for liberty. 'Rather to die as freemen, than live as slaves!' "

Brown succeeded in gaining the support of forty slaves in the area and five free blacks including Anderson, Shields Green, John Copeland, Lewis Sherrard Leary, and Danger-field Newby. Twenty-five others were on their way at the time of the attack.

The Harpers Ferry attack electrified the nation. Douglass, implicated in the plot, had to flee to Canada and England. Delany, who was also under suspicion, had already left for Africa. The Brown attack forced many white abolitionists to take a positive stand on the question of black revolutionary violence. Garrison, for instance, hailed Brown in a speech following the raid. He went on to add: "I am prepared to say, 'Success to every slave insurrection at the South, and in every slave country.' "[6]

Black opinion was nearly unanimously in support of Brown. After his execution in December, massive memorials were held in black churches throughout the North. The Union Anti-Slavery Society sponsored one of the largest at Garnet's church in New York City. Speaker after speaker rose to voice their deep admiration of Brown and his men. Garnet, delivering the principal eulogy of Brown, demanded that December 2 be designated "Martyr's Day."* He continued:

In the signs of the times, I see the dreaded truth, written as by the finger of Jehovah—"For the sins of this nation there is no atonement without the shedding of blood." If it must come O God! prepare us to meet it. The nation needed to see a picture of the future of slavery and its ends and methinks God has been pleased to draw it in crimson lines. Americans, Patriots, Christians, Tyrants, look upon it and be instructed.[7]

During the course of the event sizable contributions were received for the families of those killed at Harpers Ferry.

Undoubtedly, Garnet had responded positively to Brown

* The complete text of this eulogy is in Appendix Nine.

because he, like other blacks, saw in him the embodiment of the ideal of liberation. Brown, by literally putting into practice Garnet's earlier call for revolutionary violence, set the stage for the Civil War and so-called emancipation. W. E. B. Du Bois said in his study of Brown:

> it was true that the violence which John Brown led made Kansas a free state; that the flight of the fugitive slaves was the beginning of abolition, and the plan of John Brown to put arms in their hands could have hastened it. Although John Brown's plan failed at the time, it was actually arms and tools in the hands of a half-million Negroes that won the Civil War.[8]

Garnet was anxious to see support for abolition come from the church. At a meeting of the Evangelical Association of Colored Ministers of Congregational and Presbyterian Churches, he assailed local white churchmen for their complicity in perpetuating oppression:

> That many of the Doctors of Divinity in that city of churches, Brooklyn, did not know the definition of the word man. If they were asked to spell the word from an object, that object being a black man, they would say M–A–N, chattel or M–A–N, property.[9]

Garnet was concerned, too, that faster strides be made toward full and complete suffrage. In May 1860, he chaired the resolutions committee at the Free Suffrage Convention. The final report of the convention advocated the building of a nonpartisan campaign to pressure government officials into action on enfranchisement.

Events were now moving fast. The Brown raid and the election of Abraham Lincoln had polarized attitudes in both the North and the South. The Republican Party platform of 1860, which Lincoln campaigned on, prohibited the extension of slavery into new federal territory.

Southern planters were not prepared to accept such a provision. The survival of the plantation system required new land and accessible markets. This was a hard and fast rule for an agrarian system based on a limited number of staple crops. Herbert Aptheker explains:

> First, the system was one that required steady and swift expansion in order to live. The system existed for the purpose of realizing a profit from the sale of commodities in a world market. The rate of profit rose in direct correlation with the increase in the number of slaves employed and in the acreage tilled, especially the tilling of virginal lands, where the crops per acre rose.[10]

New land was also a requisite for the development of Southern industries, which were centered around mining, lumber, fishing, transportation, turpentine, rice milling, and sugar refining. These industries depended on slave labor. A move by the federal government to limit the acquisition of land meant a certain end to the economic growth of the South. Southern industrialists and planters believed secession was the only viable alternative.

When war was declared in April 1861, Northern blacks were the first to realize that the main issue was to be slavery. Every black leader from Garnet to Douglass instantly called for the use of black troops by the North.

Toward the end of the year, Garnet left for England to help revitalize the abolitionist movement there. Arriving in Liverpool, he began a speaking tour of the country. His major theme was that a Northern victory was necessary for the destruction of slavery. It was later acknowledged that the staunch support of British workers was a determining factor in preventing the ruling class from entering the war on the side of the Confederacy.*

---

* Under Marx's guidance, the First International waged a vigorous campaign to gain the support of English workers for the Union. In a message to Lincoln, Marx related: "The workingmen

When Garnet returned to America a year later he joined Douglass, Brown, Delany, J. M. Langston, and others in the fight to utilize black troops. Only after a string of disastrous military defeats did the government relent and change its policy on this matter. When the government began recruiting in late 1862, Garnet was hired as an agent responsible for recruitment in the New York state area. He became a member of the Black Committee, which included Douglass, Brown, and the other black recruitment agents. Their job was to raise companies of black soldiers for the Union army. The man who organized this committee and supervised the activities was George Stearns. Stearns was able to command the respect of Garnet and the other black agents because of his impeccable credentials as an abolitionist radical. He had been part of the "secret six" to aid John Brown.

Three meetings were scheduled during April 1863 at Garnet's church to recruit large numbers of black volunteers. All the appointed speakers called upon blacks to back the government in the war effort. Garnet, who chaired the meeting, was disturbed over the treatment of black troops. He insisted that blacks be upgraded to officer positions and dealt with on the same basis as whites:

> I wish to know what have black men to fight for in this war? What encouragement has been offered to them to fight? What does a soldier fight for? He fights principally for three things: love of country, promotion on the field, and for honor. What then has the black man to fight for? Under the present call of the President, a colored soldier cannot be promoted higher than a captain, a mere company officer. Are these encouragements for colored men to enlist? But I believe that if they will put a black Major-General

of Europe feel sure that, as the American War of Independence initiated a new era of ascendancy for the middle class, so the American anti-slavery war will do for the working classes."

in the field, there would be thousands of men of black skins flocking around him. But do not call the black man a coward. If he will not fight, it is because he has not justice done him. Do him justice, give him a chance equal with a white soldier, and he will show you how he can fight.[11]

At the next meeting, a week later, Garnet, Pennington, Downing, and Douglass were the featured speakers. Each one again issued an appeal for black troops. Garnet made it clear that despite the criticisms he had voiced he still fully supported the North's cause. He felt if black men did not do the same then their "doom is sealed." Basically, the same line was used by the same speakers at the final meeting that month. Garnet urged: "Join the armies of the United States, and, in the language of old John Brown, who frightened Virginia to the core, march through and through the heart of this rebellion."[12]

The pace of these meetings showed that the traditional black leaders were finally united on an issue: slavery would be crushed by the Northern army, and it was the duty of all blacks to be a part of that army. The government was praised not because of any sentimentality but because it was now regarded as an agency for liberation. Resolutions passed at the third meeting expressed this viewpoint. One stated:

Resolved, That in determination to stand by the government in this war, we are not only deciding to stand by good government, but against slavery, the parent and fosterer of the unjust prejudice we have been the subjects of here in the North. (*Douglass' Monthly*, June 1863)

In addition to his job as a recruiting agent, Garnet was an active member of the Union Loyal League Club. Under this group's sponsorship, he served as chaplain to two regiments of black troops formed in New York.

Altogether, about two hundred twenty thousand blacks served as soldiers in the Union army; another twenty-five thousand were in the navy. A quarter of a million were employed by the army as teamsters, scouts, cooks, nurses, and fortification and railroad builders. Lincoln later acknowledged that blacks had provided the decisive force that led to the North's victory. Blacks were far in advance of the government in recognizing the radical implications of the war for the future. According to William Z. Foster:

> Among the several elements on the left were the Negro people themselves. They were the most definitely revolutionary of any of the groups or classes in the Civil War period. This was true of both the slaves in the South and of the freedmen and women in the North. There were several basic planks in their general program, as formulated in the North, including: (a) the emancipation of the slaves; (b) the arming of the Negro slaves and freedmen; (c) the enfranchisement of the Negro people; (d) the abolition of Jim Crow and social inequality; (e) the redistribution of the land in the South. . . . The degree of revolutionary content in the Federal Government's policy was always measured by the extent to which it adopted and was enforcing the national demands of the Negro people.[13]

The black population clearly swung the pendulum of support toward emancipation. Blacks urged Lincoln to free the slaves long before it had occurred to the government that this could be a practical weapon against the South. During the summer of 1862, when Lincoln finally announced that he intended to issue a proclamation as a limited war measure to free slaves in certain areas, blacks were the first to respond. On September 29, a mass meeting was held at Garnet's church to praise Lincoln. Addressing the audience, Garnet recounted his personal experiences as a slave on a Maryland plantation. He closed with the demand that Lincoln uphold his pledge.

The war was by no means uniformly supported by Northern whites. Because of their deep racism, many whites wanted no part of anything that would contribute to black freedom. In July 1863, this resentment erupted into violence in New York City. Whites, particularly recent immigrants, openly attacked the city's blacks. The immediate issue was the conscription act Congress had enacted to provide more men for the Union army. The riots were no surprise to many. A number of white merchants were heavily dependent on trade with the South. It was estimated that New York businessmen received nearly forty cents out of each dollar paid for Southern cotton. In 1859 alone, merchandise valued at $131 million had been sold to Southerners by these businessmen. New York shipbuilders also had long specialized in providing transport for the slave traders. The climate for the riots was created by these businessmen, who, as a result of their economic ties, identified strongly with the Southern cause.

The riots lasted five days and claimed the lives of hundreds of blacks; thousands of others were left homeless. Garnet, widely known throughout New York, was a target of the white mobs. He escaped injury only when his daughter took the name plate off the door of his residence.

When order was restored by federal troops sent into the city, a Committee of Merchants for the Relief of Colored People was formed to aid the victims. The committee appointed Garnet, Ray, and three other black ministers to investigate the claims of the riot victims and determine how they should be assisted. Eventually, more than $40,000 was collected for a relief fund set up by the committee. During August, the committee, under Garnet's direction, aided more than six thousand people.

In appreciation, the leading black ministers of New York City issued an address, which Garnet wrote, thanking the merchants who had contributed for their help. The address also stated:

> If, in your temporary labors of Christian philanthropy, you have been induced to look forward to our future destiny in this our native land, and to ask what is the best thing that we can do for the colored people, this is our answer:—Protect us in our endeavors to obtain an honest living—suffer no one to hinder us in any department of well-directed industry, give us a fair and open field and let us work out our own destiny, and we ask no more.[14]

Even though the merchants' committee was held in high esteem, the general feeling was that the black community must assume the burden for its own reconstruction and growth.

In April 1864, Garnet moved from New York City to Washington, D.C., where he became pastor of the Fifteenth Street Presbyterian Church. By this time, the tide of battle had turned in favor of the North. Union armies had captured most of the South's key areas and were preparing for the final assault against the main strongholds of Southern power in Virginia.

As the war was drawing to an end, in February 1865, Garnet was invited by Rev. William H. Channing, chaplain of the House of Representatives, to deliver a sermon to the House. The first black ever asked to preach there, Garnet was the center of attention in Washington for days before the event. On the scheduled day, February 12, many of the city's blacks and government officials packed the galleries to hear him speak.

Garnet based his sermon on Matthew 23:4, about the Scribes and the Pharisees who say one thing and do another.* The sermon reflected a number of the ideals Garnet had fought for over the years. He chose to reiterate

* The complete text of this sermon is in Appendix Ten.

his support of Africa: "Go to the shores of the land of my forefathers, poor bleeding Africa, which, although she has been bereaved, and robbed for centuries, is nevertheless beloved by all her worthy descendants wherever dispersed."[15] He anticipated the thirteenth, fourteenth, and fifteenth amendments to the Constitution by calling for the government to eradicate slavery from its national life and to "Emancipate, Enfranchise, and Educate" every American citizen.

After his discourse, the elders and trustees of his church adopted resolutions commending Congress for giving Garnet the opportunity to speak. They also praised the abolitionist movement and authorized the publication of the speech with an account of Garnet's life by James Mc-Cune Smith.

Garnet was supporting a drive to secure relief for black troops who had been discharged from the army and were destitute. To raise money he had formed a group known as the Colored Soldier's Aid Society. The society held two meetings at his church. Sojourner Truth was a featured speaker at one of them. In a conversation with her, Garnet expressed his disappointment over the government's failure to meet the needs of Washington's black population:

> The free colored people of Washington have always had to pay city taxes, like other citizens, but the city would never let our children go to the schools supported by our taxes. So we started our own schools and paid our own teachers. We took care of our own poor, too, until the freedmen started pouring into the city. There are three times as many colored people in the city now as there were before the war, and most of them are in terrible need. We can't possibly take care of all these ourselves. We're swamped.[16]

After the assassination of Lincoln in April 1865, Garnet became president of the National Lincoln Monument Association. The organization wanted to erect a statue in

Lincoln's memory with funds collected from the black community. The life directors of the group included Delany, Loguen, Robert Hamilton, Daniel A. Payne, William Whipple, and James McCune Smith.

The association appealed directly to black organizations such as the Masonic and Odd Fellows societies, benevolent associations, churches, and Sabbath schools for contributions. Garnet sent letters to friends soliciting money for the monument. On July 4, the association held a celebration in Washington. Letters of support were received from white notables such as Salmon P. Chase, Gerrit Smith, John C. Fremont, and Charles Sumner. In a speech, Howard Day praised the heroism of black soldiers in the Civil War and called for a renewed commitment to the struggle for freedom.

A few blacks objected to the National Lincoln Monument Association. They felt that the group was being too narrow in working principally among blacks. Douglass agreed with this position. In a letter declining the association's offer of the vice-presidency for the state of New York, Douglass wrote:

> When we wish to build tombstones or monuments of any kind, in our own name, as a class, let us build them with our own money, and if we have to build monuments with white men's money let us by all means have the grace to admit that the monument is as much the property of the whites as of the blacks, and has no more right to be called a colored people's than a white people's monument.[17]

Garnet, deeply offended by Douglass' remarks, announced the association's intention to carry on its work and to become incorporated under the laws of the District of Columbia. Garnet also chided Douglass for opposing the raising of money for a planned institute for the education of blacks:

If an attempt is to be made to defeat a noble effort to educate the rising generations of the South, in which you and I were born slaves, for heaven's sake let not the ignoble work be undertaken by a negro.[18]

Garnet then added:

After we build the Lincoln Monument Institute and appoint able profesors, black and white, we hope to work further South and build another to the memory of "old John Brown of Ossawatomie," and his nineteen black compatriots who fell at Harpers Ferry, and who set the great ball in motion that crushed out the devilish life of slavery.[19]

In July, Garnet officially joined the staff of the *Weekly Anglo-African* as an editor in charge of the Southern department. In the same month he left on a four-month tour of the South. The trip was undertaken mainly to gather information through personal observation of post-war conditions of Southern blacks. The first stop on his trip was New Market, Maryland, where he had been born into slavery. While there, he conversed with a number of former slaveholders and "was most kindly received by them." According to him, they "actually seemed to be quite proud that even a black man, a native of Kent, received some little consideration from his fellow men."[20] His travels took him from Kent to St. Louis, where he reported, "My journey has been a most pleasant one thus far. Everywhere my friends welcome me."[21]

In nearly every town Garnet visited, the local black residents asked him to speak. Typical was his reception in Richmond, Virginia. He recorded these impressions of entering the city:

In approaching the city through the sluggish red and muddy waters of the James river, we make our way

among the remains of exploded steamers and iron-
clads, that look like huge alligators basking in the
sun. God has erected many a monument of His retri-
butive justice in the waters and along the shores of
that river, so famous in history for bearing on its
bosom the first cargo of African slaves brought to this
country, and also for being the first to hear the
triumphant shouts of the black soldiers, descendants
of those very ancestors, some two hundred and forty
years after, when this rebel capital tumbled into
ruins.

Fifteen hundred of the finest stores and mills are
in ruins. Five hundred colored men are at work
clearing away rubbish and the rich men are sitting
in sackcloth and ashes. The angel of death and
desolation has swept over this once proud and beautiful city.[22]

During the several days he was there he made the
rounds of the black churches. Garnet was also requested
to speak at a mass meeting that was being held to appoint
delegates to the upcoming Virginia State Convention.

Garnet made careful notes about the effects of Reconstruction. He entirely supported the freedmen's demand
for land and the franchise. He considered them the real
basis for building a just and democratic society in the
South. They would act as a bulwark against the return to
power of the former planters. The success of Reconstruction, he often repeated, depended greatly on the division
and equitable distribution among blacks of the former
planters' lands. Many freedmen, though, were not content
to sit idly by, placing their hopes in Washington. In some
areas, they seized the estates abandoned by their masters
during the war. According to James S. Allen:

In a number of home colonies the Negroes set up a
form of self-government and in some places worked
the land on a cooperative basis. . . . Even before the

armed combat reached a decisive conclusion, the former slaves were already reaching out eagerly for all the benefits of democracy.[23]

During his travels, Garnet concluded that the government was moving neither fast enough nor far enough on the land question.* He confided to Gerrit Smith that the plan of Reconstruction "may be disastrous to the cause of freedom."[24] He thought that President Johnson was backsliding on all the promises that the government had made to the freedmen.

In October, he wound up his tour and returned to Washington. He announced in the *Weekly Anglo-African* that he would as soon as possible publish the findings of his trip as a pamphlet in order to elicit more aid for the freedmen.

In January 1866, Garnet presided over a special convention at his church to discuss the problems of Reconstruction. Those assembled were especially concerned over the pending legislation dealing with civil rights, the Freedmen's Bureau, and the Fourteenth Amendment. They backed each of these measures and urged the government to "guarantee and secure to all loyal citizens, irrespective of race or color, equal rights before the law, including the right of impartial suffrage.[25]

Although he never accepted a post in the Freedmen's Bureau, Garnet did work closely with the various freedmen's aid societies formed in several Northern cities. In Washington the most important black societies were the

---

* T. Thomas Fortune mentions this in his *Black and White: Land, Labor and Politics in the South* (New York, 1884). To prevent the rich and propertied in the South from again controlling government it was mandatory that the "system of land monopoly be destroyed." Fortune continued:

> The landlord simply stands out as the representative of the real grievance. To remove him would not remove the evil; agitation would not cease; murder would still stalk abroad at noonday. *The real grievance is the false system which makes the landlord possible.*

Contraband Relief Association and the Union Relief Association of Israel Bethel Church (A.M.E.). The Contraband Committee of Mother Bethel Church, in Philadelphia, and the Freedmen's Friend Society of Brooklyn were also significant. Even Garnet's old organization, the African Civilization Society, established a few schools for freedmen in Washington.[26]

During the next few years, Garnet was persistent in his demands that the government provide the freedmen with land and uphold their political rights. He recognized that the former slaves needed the means to develop their land. In an address before the Freedmen's Aid Society in Pittsburgh, in November 1866, he declared:

> we black people . . . do not intend to be crushed out, we do not intend to die beneath the oppressor's heel. We feel that we have God and all good men on our side. We have in us the Phoenix's spirit which though buried in ashes cries from those ashes, "I will arise," and springs up to new and vigorous life. Give us school houses, give us churches, and if this shall be done, if the Northern people shall do this, then— and not till then—shall your light break forth as the morning.[27]

During the 1870's, Garnet attempted to maintain contact with people once active in the abolitionist movement. In 1869, he had attended a national Negro convention in Washington, D.C., and presided as convention chairman. In 1870, he was on the podium with Douglass and others at the last meeting of the American Anti-Slavery Society. Back in New York City again as pastor of the Shiloh Presbyterian Church, he was constantly asked for advice on the problems confronting blacks. Douglass, in 1874, sought his opinion about the viability and soundness of the Freedman's Savings and Trust Company. Garnet also took a special interest in the government's operations and in its relation to black people. He personally thanked one admirer who had sent him copies of the pamphlets *Amendments to the Constitution of the United States* and *Organization of Colored Troops and the Regeneration of the South.*[28]

Another issue that drew his attention was the plight of blacks in Cuba. During the early 1870's, a small movement for Cuban independence had begun to grow among Afro-Americans. The key to emancipation on the island was the overthrow of Spanish rule. The movement had the support of Douglass, Downing, P. B. S. Pinchback, the black lieutenant governor of Louisiana, and other black spokesmen. Garnet organized a Cuban Anti-Slavery Committee in early 1873 and served as the group's secretary. The committee collected five thousand signatures on petitions, which it presented to Congress and to President Grant at the White House. In a speech to the delegation, Grant assured the committee that he sympathized with the condition of the Cubans and that his Cabinet would give the matter further consideration. When no official action was taken on the petitions, Garnet and other members of the committee proclaimed their displeasure. The Cuban Anti-Slavery Committee was clearly bucking the tide. The government had no intention of intervening in Cuba to protect black interests. The United States wanted to end Spanish domination of the island, but for reasons far different from those of the committee. To exploit the island's tremendous sugar resources, the United States two decades later precipitated war with Spain and grabbed not only Cuba, but Puerto Rico, and the Philippines as well.

On the home front, Garnet became increasingly alarmed over the growing repression of Southern blacks. He protested the government's lack of interest in the problems of the freedmen. He realized that Reconstruction was a giant failure. Northern industrialists had used the freedmen as pawns to gain political and economic ascendancy over the former planter class. This clique now completely controlled the national government at the expense of blacks in the South. Howard Zinn asserts:

"Radical Reconstruction" was not based on genuine Negro power, but on the Negro's usefulness—for a while—to Northern politicians. By the second Grant administration it was becoming clear to the dominant forces in the North that the road to their own prosperity and power did not lie in Negro suffrage. Businessmen and politicians needed domestic tranquility more than anything else, and this could only be secured with the cooperation of the white elite of the South.[29]

Although some aspects of Reconstruction provided temporary benefits to blacks and poor whites in the South, there were many more setbacks than gains. Reconstruction failed simply because it was never intended to succeed. When blacks had served their purpose, they were quickly discarded.

When this happened, many Southern blacks again began to look toward Africa. Emigrationist sentiment once again flowered. In 1878, the *Azor* sailed from Charleston, South Carolina, with a group of black emigrants. Leaders such as Henry M. Turner issued vigorous calls for an exodus to Africa, and in several cities emigration organizations were formed.

Garnet began to make plans for a trip to Liberia. He had told friends that he wanted to be buried on the African continent. In May 1881, his daughter left for Liberia to found a women's school under the auspices of the Ladies Board of Missions of the Presbyterian Church. Later in the year, Garnet was appointed United States minister resident and consul general to Liberia. Leaving New York City, he arrived in Monrovia in early January 1882. Shortly after his arrival, he was feted at a dinner by Edward Wilmot Blyden, who was the president of Liberia College. In all, seventy people attended the dinner, including Liberian cabinet officers, legislators, the chief justice, and foreign dignitaries. Garnet took the occasion to praise the progress Liberians had made in building a nation.

Garnet had contracted the fever on his arrival, but after a few days of rest he felt well enough to visit his daughter, whose school was fourteen miles from Monrovia. Immediately after returning from the visit, he suffered an asthma attack. Still weakened by the fever, he was unable to regain his strength. Garnet died on the morning of February 12, 1882, at the age of sixty-six. He was given a state funeral, and every Liberian official was present. The eulogy was read by Blyden. Garnet was buried at Palm Grove Cemetery, which overlooks the Atlantic.

Tributes poured in from individuals and groups in America that had either known or heard of his work. In several black churches in the North, memorial services were held in his honor. The Presbytery of New York passed a resolution on April 10, 1882, which said in part:

> That his death as he was just entering upon his duties as Minister to Liberia, where he had a wide field for the exercise of his talents, and where he promised to be greatly useful, is to be deplored as a calamity to that republic and to the colored race (Alexander Crummell, *Eulogium on Henry Highland Garnet in America and Africa* [Springfield, Mass., 1891], p. 298).

In acknowledging his debt to Garnet for his life of struggle for the cause of black liberation, Henry M. Turner perhaps best expressed the feelings of many in a letter written from Liberia several years later:

> For forty years before Mr. Lincoln issued his proclamation of freedom, Dr. Garnet fought for his race as no other man could, except Douglass, when the lips of the Southern negro were sealed and he was gored by the slave masters to the verge of death. Dr. Garnet periled life and everything for his freedom.[30]

Conclusion

William Pickens once remarked that the abolitionist movement began with the flight of the first fugitive slave. This
is true. Out of the ranks of the fugitives came the black
abolitionists. These men and women influenced the course
of American history in the nineteenth century.

Garnet certainly was a key member of this circle. He
took an advanced position on all issues of vital concern to
blacks. His speeches in 1842 and 1843 were brilliant
statements on the causes and consequences of the black
struggle. In company with Delany and others, Garnet
gave black nationalism a theoretical and political dimen-
sion, which it previously had lacked. He recognized that
only through the development of an independent power
base could the black liberation movement progress. The
participation of white abolitionists in the anti-slavery organizations would not assure the success of these groups.
They had to be completely under the control of blacks.
Garnet continually stressed this.

From the 1840's on, increasing numbers of blacks sub-
scribed to this view. After 1850, nearly all were looking
toward the black world. Nation building was emphasized
because it seemed to be a means of exerting leverage
against the institutions of oppression in the West and
because independent black nations would increase the
world's respect for Afro-Americans.

Garnet's opposition to moral suasion, nonviolence, the

rich and propertied, and his support for political action, the redistribution of land, and slave rebellions had a lasting effect on the abolitionist movement. Many similarities exist between the black movement of the nineteenth century and today's struggle. Blacks continue to demand land, power, and the right to self-defense. In some instances, even the slogans are identical. The leaders of the early period were masters of the art of confrontation politics. Self-sacrifice and dedication to the cause of black freedom were integral to their existence. Like freedom fighters today, Garnet never sought personal comfort or gain. He once remarked that because of his beliefs "he had been a poor man all his life." It was no coincidence that Michael (Cetewayo) Tabor of the Black Panther Party invoked Garnet's name during a speech at an anti-repression rally in New York City. This was a gratifying tribute to the progressive leadership Garnet brought to the black movement.

Just as in the 1850's organizations such as vigilance committees, emigration associations, and national emigration conventions arose, so today we see a similar development with the emergence of groups like the Panthers, the League of Revolutionary Black Workers, and Black Student Unions. Like their forerunners they grew as a direct response to the rising political and racial consciousness of blacks.

Garnet and others saw that economic exploitation was a major problem facing blacks. Although he did not analyze the system of capitalism from a "scientific socialist" position (Marxism had not made any appreciable impact on American society in the ante-bellum period), he perceived that black oppression was closely connected with the dominance of a wealthy landowning class.

The black church in the immediate pre–Civil War period helped initiate positive social change. The leadership of many black ministers was decisive in building the abolitionist movement. Ministers such as Garnet not only talked about liberation but acted on it as well. Shiloh

Presbyterian Church remained open day and night for meetings, for housing fugitive slaves, for providing for the needy. To Garnet, the gospel of freedom took precedence over everything. Heaven meant nothing if black men could not enjoy its fruits on earth. It is no overstatement to say that Malcolm X would have felt at home in Garnet's church.

Because of his stand on these questions, Garnet was one of the most controversial men in America. He was often criticized by both blacks and whites. Nevertheless, no matter how sharp the disagreement, he retained their respect. It was of little concern to him that he had been poor all his life because of his ideas. His reward came when blacks were freed from chattel slavery.

Garnet was truly a pioneer black liberationist. His role as an early anti-war, anti-monopoly wealth, and black liberationist holds tremendous meaning for today's radical movement. It is imperative that this man's speeches and writings be read and studied. Important lessons can be drawn from his life—lessons that could have great bearing for the liberation struggle today. The conditions that presently confront blacks are not too qualitatively different from those of a century ago.

Everyone concerned with finding just solutions to the problems of racism and exploitation should at some point let their motto be resistance.

Appendix: Selected Speeches and Writings of Henry Highland Garnet

1.

SPEECH DELIVERED AT THE SEVENTH ANNIVERSARY OF THE AMERICAN ANTI-SLAVERY SOCIETY, 1840

Resolved, That all the rights and immunities of American citizens are justly due to the people of color, who have ever been, and still are, willing to contribute their full share to enrich and to defend our common country.

In rising, Mr. President, to bespeak the passage of the resolution which I have just read, I cannot hope to express all the feelings of my heart. I would point this assembly to the early history of our country. I would invite Americans to examine anew the foundations of our republican institutions. I would remind you, sir, of dear-bought privileges said to be held out to all, but which are, notwithstanding, denied to immortal millions. I would hold up before you covenants written with blood, that might have been placed in the ark of the nation's glory, but which have been seized by the oppressor's hand, and torn to pieces by his scourge. I would call you to listen to the shrill sound of the plantation horn, that comes leaping from the South, and finding an echo even among our northern hills. In a word, I would direct your attention to a pile of wrong, and national disgrace, and shame, as high as heaven.

Sir, the foundation of this government was formed of the most solid materials. Those who first laid their hands to the work of building up in this new world an edifice within whose walls the most extensive liberty should abide, were men who had no communion with tyranny and oppression. It must ever animate and cheer the bosom of the true American patriot, to dwell upon the moral sublimity of the spirit of the pilgrims—a spirit which led them to break asunder the ties that bound them to kindred and country, and to fix their dwellings, and to throw their destinies in the midst of the trackless wilderness. While speaking of those men, the tongue of the orator will never become ineloquent. The strains of the poet that shall entwine their deeds in song, shall never vex the ear of patriotism. As they launched into the deep, their very sails were swelled by the breath of liberty. As pure in motive and as resistless in spirit as the waves that bore them thither, they laid the broad foundation of republican institutions. It was then, sir, that new and astonishing truths in regard to the principles of liberty were developed. Acting under the influence of these truths, *our* fathers pressed forward with holy and patriotic zeal in the road to that national independence which the revolution of '76 opened to them. Of the wonderful perseverence—of the ceaseless love of liberty, religious, political, and social, which regulated their actions, who is so base as to complain?

Of the principles laid down in the Declaration of Independence, we find no fault. For that instrument declares, "that all men are created free and equal." We would not question the sincerity of purpose, and devotion to freedom, which seemed to wield the swords of most of the fathers of the revolution. But we complain, in the most unqualified terms, of the base conduct of their degenerate sons. If, when taking into consideration the circumstances with which the revolutionists were surrounded, and the weakness of human nature, we can possibly pardon them for neglecting our brethren's rights—if, in the first dawning of the day of liberty, every part of the patriot's duty did not appear plain, now that we have reached the mid-day of our national career—now that there are ten thousand suns flashing light upon our pathway, this nation is guilty of the basest hypocrisy in withholding the rights due to millions of American citizens.

It is not necessary, Mr. President, for me to attempt to mark out the grounds upon which is built the right of American citizenship. Let it be what it may, upon it the colored inhabitants of this country stand.

It is with pride that I remember, that in the earliest attempts to establish democracy in this hemisphere, colored men stood by the side of your fathers, and shared with them the toils of the revolution. When freedom, that had been chased over half the world, at last thought she had here found a shelter, and held out her hands for protection, the tearful eye of the colored man, in many instances, gazed with pity upon her tattered garments, and ran to her relief. Many fell in her defence. The grateful soil received them affectionately into its bosom. No monumental piles distinguish their "dreamless beds." Scarcely an inch on the page of history has been appropriated to their memory. Yet truth will give them a share of the fame that was reaped upon the field of Lexington and Bunker Hill. Truth will affirm that they participated in the immortal honor that adorned the brow of the illustrious Washington.

In the last war, also, the colored citizens rendered signal service to the country. So anxious were they to defend their native shores from invasion, at the battle of New Orleans, that they did not stop to consult the safety of General Jackson's cotton bags. In order to show to you their ardor in that struggle, permit me to recite to you the words of the late President of the United States: "I knew well how you loved your native country, and that you had, as well as ourselves, to defend what man holds most dear—parents, relations, wives, children, and property.

You have done more than I expected. In addition to those previous qualities I before knew you to possess, I found, moreover, among you a noble enthusiasm which leads to the performance of great things." Such is the language of slaveholders when they would have colored men stand in the front of battle. If they are forgotten by history—if they are not mentioned in the halls of Congress—if prejudice denies them a place in the grateful recollections of Americans in general, I trust they will at least be remembered amid the cloister of the Hermitage.

Sir, in consideration of the toils of our fathers in both wars, we claim the right of American citizenship. We claim it, but shall we ever enjoy it? Our ancestors fought and bled for it, but I will leave it with this assembly to decide, whether they fought and bled as wise men or as fools. They have gone to their rest, many of them with their brows all marked with wounds received in fighting the battles of liberty, while their backs were furrowed by the cruel scourge. Unfortunate men!—They knew not that their children were to be immolated upon the altars of slavery—altars erected upon their very graves. They little thought that the power against which they were fighting would one day emancipate all its slaves, while their own country would master all her power, and make her mightiest effort to blot out the few scattering stars that linger in the horizon of their posterity's hopes.

But what shall be said? Shall we blame these men, and say that they slew their own interests? No, sir, if the revolution was right, they have done nobly, and will stand approved of heaven in the last great day. For, seeing this self same soil which now yields the bitter fruits of slavery in such abundance, in days that have passed, yielded other fruits, "we ought to blame the culture, not the soil."

In the exercise of religion, Mr. President, which is the salt that has kept the nation from moral putrefaction, the people of color have rendered their fellow-citizens some small assistance. Our religion, truly, has taught us to cling to that charity which suffereth long, and endureth all things.

The truthfulness of the words of the British statesmen, that religion is the basis of civil society, is almost universally acknowledged. And the spirit of our institutions lays it down as a primary duty of Americans, to acknowledge the moral government of God in all our affairs. The greatest blessings which we have received as a nation, have been given unto us on account of the little piety that has been found among us. And no one will say that there has not been now and then a pious soul among our people, although there is enough sin among us to excite the tears of the Christian world. The spirit of Christianity, while it is as extensive as the universe in its desire to do good to man, it is also as impartial as the light of heaven. It does not stop to consider the complexion of its adorers. No fervent prayer of the righteous has ever fallen to the earth. No stone brought up to build altars to God, by hands however humble, has ever been rejected. He who heareth the ravens when they cry, and feedeth the young lion when he roars for lack of food, most assuredly forgets not the petitions of his chosen people.

Religion, then, is the preservation of our institutions. It is the mighty pillar which holds up the well begun structure of this government, which I trust it will ultimately finish. Colored men have been with you in this labor. We are with you still, and will be with you forever. We even hope to worship in the earthly temples of our Lord. If they finally fall as did the Churches of Asia, on account of their sins, without being guilty of contributing to their destruction, let us be buried beneath their ruins. We wish not to survive their overthrow.

Sir, the slaveholder looks upon his victim as though he were not an heir of immortality. The apologists of oppression disregard his tears and blood. Church and state, the one holding up a Christianity, falsely so called, immersed in blood, and the other endeavoring to shield itself behind law, have united in platting a scourge, with which they have whipped him away from the highest privileges, and driven him into the most hopeless darkness. But from the gloom of the dungeon, prayers, fervent, righteous prayers, have ascended, in answer to which are the blessings that we now enjoy. Among the slaves of the South, have been found some of the Lots, in consideration of whose supplications, the Lord of Hosts has turned back the fiery waves of the vengeance which a disregard of His law in high places has justly merited.

Sir, if the privilege of American citizenship is granted in return for services done in contributing to the agricultural prosperity of the country, what class of Americans stands above the colored inhabitants of the soil? Who is it that will deny that they here stand pre-eminently entitled to the blessings of life and liberty? Let America blush with eternal shame, and hang her guilty head, when it is fearlessly asserted, that many of our poor, unfortunate females, bleeding under the lash of monsters, have been and still are the tillers of the land. From the Chesapeake Bay to the Sabine river, there is not a foot of cultivated ground that has not smiled beneath the hard hand of the dark American. In the middle States also, we have contributed our proportionate share in tilling the soil. But the South, that points to her cotton fields and sugar plantations, that luxuriates in her orange groves fanned by her spicy breezes, that exults in the pride of her mighty rivers, the South, that boasts of her slave supported hospitality, and manages to scare half the world by the blaze of her chivalry, and who in her turn is frightened into hysterics at the appearance of that awful raw-head-and-bloody-bones that is continually groaning, "can't take care of themselves," she is indebted to us for every breath of agricultural prosperity that she draws. Hear slaveholders themselves on the subject. If we emancipate our slaves, say they, we are undone. Without stopping to show the fallacy of a part of their doctrine, I would have you notice the bare fact set forth in this language, that so far as the agricultural interests of the South are concerned, the slave is her all in all. And, indeed, not only in the labor of the field are the people of color her bone and sinew, her life and blood, for we are told by one who knows all about the wholesome and industrious influence of slavery, that Southern republicans, in case emancipation should take place, would be put to their wit's end as to how their boots should be blacked.

If the dwellers beyond the Potomac have any thing to boast of, it is the wealth of their fields.—It is here among the rocks and valleys of the North, that the trades display their ten thousand implements. The very clothing in which these dealers in the souls of men are dressed, and the carriages in which they ride, are made at the North. The bowie knives which they flourish in Quixotic glory, are manufactured in New York, or somewhere else among innocent Northerners. The whips that they bury in the quivering flesh of their prostrate victims, are platted on the banks of the Passaic. Since the first captive was landed on the old Dominions, colored men have been toiling to make the South what she is to-day.

Not only in war, and in the exercise of religion, and in promoting the agricultural interests of the country, have colored men assisted you, but they have also contributed greatly in supporting the science and literature of the South. For poor Tom and Dick are sold far away in order that my young lord Frederick William may be sent to college.

Sir, it has been shown, that we assisted you in the days that tried men's souls. We have knelt with you on the footstool of our Heavenly Father, and have supplicated with you for blessings, civil, religious, and political. And may God grant that we may never be behind any class of our fellow-citizens in this respect. In slavery we have greatly aided in turning your wildernesses into fruitful fields. Give us our freedom, remunerate us for our labor, and protect our family altars, and, by the blessings of heaven, we will help make those fruitful fields to blossom, and bloom as Eden.

With every fibre of our hearts entwined around our country, and with an indefeasible determination to obtain the possession of the natural and inalienable rights of

American citizens, we demand redress for the wrongs we have suffered, and ask for the restoration of our birth-right privileges.—But we would not look to man alone for these things. The Lord is our strength.

> Avenge thy plundered poor, O Lord!
> But not with fire, but not with sword;
> Avenge our wrongs, our chains, our sighs,
> The misery in our children's eyes!
>   But not with sword—no, not with fire,
> Chastise our country's locustry;
>   Nor let them feel thine heavier ire;
> Chastise them not in poverty;
>   Though cold in soul as coffined dust,
> Their hearts as tearless, dead, and dry,
>   Let them in outraged mercy trust,
> And find that mercy they deny.

I speak in the behalf of my enslaved brethren and the nominally free. There is, Mr. President, a higher sort of freedom, which no mortal can touch. That freedom, thanks be unto the Most High, is mine. Yet I am not, nay, cannot be entirely free. I feel for my brethren as a man—I am bound with them as a brother. Nothing but emancipating my brethren can set me at liberty. If that greatest of all earthly blessings, "prized above all price," cannot be found in my own native land, then I must be a stranger to it during my pilgrimage here below. For although I were dwelling beneath the bright skies of Asia, or listening to the harp-like strains of the gentle winds that whisper of free-dom among the groves of Africa—though my habitation were fixed in the freest part of Victoria's dominions, yet it were vain, and worse than vain for me to indulge the thought of being free, while three millions of my country-men are wailing in the dark prison-house of oppression.

In submitting the resolution, sir, I would again call upon Americans to remember, that but a few years ago, their fathers crossed the ocean in search of the freedom now denied to us. I would beseech them to remember that the great day of God's final reckoning is just before us, remember his eternal justice, and then remember the outcast bondman, and let him go forth free in the presence of God, in whose image he was created.

2.

REPORT ON THE BEST MEANS FOR THE PROMOTION OF THE ENFRANCHISEMENT OF OUR PEOPLE, SCHENECTADY, 1844

The committee have been brief in their report, so that its length might not be an objection to its perusal.

A resort to no one class of means could remove the disabilities which obstruct our improvement, but it requires a happy combination of all laudable pursuits to secure such an end. Yet there are some particular pursuits which would tend more than others to remove the prejudice which a majority of our fellow-citizens cherish towards us. We proceed to name some of the most prominent and available.

1. A general diffusion of literary, scientific and religious knowledge among the people. This can be done, as it has already been done in some places, by the establishment of Public Libraries, Lyceums, and Public Lectures.

2. By the careful education of our youth, and holding out to them additional encouragement, in proportion to the extra difficulties which they have to encounter.

3. By giving our children useful trades, and by patronizing those who may have engaged in useful handicrafts.

4. The committee would urge as first in importance the removal of our people from the cities and large towns, and the betaking of themselves to the country. Prejudice is so strong in cities, and custom is so set and determined, that it is impossible for us to emerge from the most laborious and the least profitable occupations.

For instance, in the city of New York, a colored citizen

cannot obtain a license to drive a cart! Many such like inconveniences beset them on every hand. Thus scores of men, whose intelligence (we would say nothing of their enterprise) is sufficient to entitle them to stations of trust and profit, are compelled to drudge out their lives for a scanty subsistence. It has been seen, that when they have satisfied the demands of the landlord, provided their fuel, and have paid devotion to the shrine of fashion, there is nothing left for "a rainy day," and they often die in want.

Not so in the country, where every man is known, and even our people who are so much abused in cities are respected almost according to their moral worth. The committee would not say that there are none of these difficulties in the country—but that there are far less than are met with in cities, we do affirm.

In the country, no man is prohibited from driving a cart! Nay, he can raise his own horses and cattle, and drive them over his fruitful fields, or to the fair, or to the market, or elsewhere. He can go to the woods and get his fuel, and burn the same in his log cabin, when winter winds are abroad, without fearing lest his solid comfort should be interrupted by a surly landlord, who is as certain to come every three months, as death is at the end of life.

In the towns of Syracuse and Geneva, among a colored population of some eight hundred, there are more voters according to the odious $250 qualification, than there are in New York City, which has eighteen or twenty thousand colored inhabitants.

Whoever will take the pains to examine facts on the subject, will find that real influence and property dwindles away in the hands of our people, as we approach cities and large towns. In New York City there is but one* instance among our High Schools, Theological Seminaries, and Colleges, in which a colored youth can avail himself of its benefits. In many other cities not even one exception is found.

Indeed, the Committee know of no College or Female

* Union Theological Seminary.

Seminary in any city of the Union whose doors are open for our children.

If the talents of our young men, which in the cities are hindered in their growth, were transplanted to the country, there is no prejudice so strong as to be able to roll back the tide of our enfranchisement.*

In every prosperous country, and among every powerful and influential people, whose territory would admit of the employment, agriculture has contributed its full share of wealth and glory. In our country, where labor is honorable, and where the fruitful earth invites the husbandman to dress and till it, agriculture is emphatically the surest road to temporal happiness.

In the proudest days of Rome, when she stretched out her sceptre over a subjugated world, she called her favorite from the furrowed field. Her legislators encouraged her farmers, nor did the sun of her glory begin to set, until her fields were neglected, and her sons exchanged that honorable labor for the luxury and licentiousness of cities and camps. The Committee would venture to say, that if agriculture bore such an important part in promoting the greatness of an entire nation, the same course would secure an influence for the oppressed portion of any people.

But every man that removes to the country, or to some small and growing town, need not necessarily become a farmer. If he be a mechanic, he may turn his attention to his trade, with great advantage. Cities are not in themselves unfavorable to our people, but public opinion in them is such as to render it next to impossible for us to rise above dependence. Let our men become the owners of the soil, and they shall be the founders of towns and villages; and as they grow up, they may grow with them,

---

* A member of the Committee was a short time ago informed by the esteemed Governor of Massachusetts, that there is a humble, though upright colored citizen of his town, who is doing more by his example and intelligence to benefit his people, than all other human efforts. He would not have been noticed in a large city.

and may give tone and character to a just and liberal public sentiment.

Let a few families select a good spot, having favorable water privileges, and other advantages—let them subdue the forests, erect their mills, and build their workshops, and in a few years they will have a thriving village. Or let them go to some youthful towns just springing into existence.

In conclusion the Committee would advise families and individuals to leave the large cities, and repair to the country, and by observing the other recommendations in the report, they will use the best and most certain means to promote our happiness and enfranchisement.

3.

SPEECH DELIVERED AT THE LIBERTY PARTY
CONVENTION, MASSACHUSETTS, 1842

Mr. President, in rising to address this assembly, on the great question of slavery, I feel what I cannot find language to express. When I consider the millions of my fellow men that are now groaning under the chains of slavery, the tyranny of their oppressors, and the apathy of the North on this subject, I hardly know where to begin or where to end. But in no way could I address you more to the purpose than to call your attention to the resolution which I hold in my hand.

It is argued by many that we are "pursuing a wrong course," in carrying our principles out at the polls, but sir, for one, I have no fears on that point; let time, that is called "the touchstone of character to man," show to future generations the course we pursued in 1842; they will award to us *consistency* in our conduct, honesty of purpose, and entire devotedness to the cause of holy and impartial freedom. (*Hear, hear.*)

The opposition which the friends of Liberty have had to encounter, in advocating the cause of the oppressed, has been overruled by God, who is the author of good, for the furtherance of the principles they maintain, and the spread of freedom. The abolitionists are not of those who are enervated in the germ and blossom of life, and dandled on the downy lap of prosperity to inglorious repose; but as the historian remarked of Philip, from those adverse fortunes which could not break their spirits, they have learned patience, humility and wisdom; they have found ample resources in their own minds made strong by *exertion* and rich by *experience*. (*Loud cheering.*)

But sir, far be it from us to ascribe the glory to ourselves. All our success is of God, "who raiseth up one nation and putteth down another"; yes, that Almighty Being who said, "let there be light and there was light," has called into being the Spirit of this age, to bring out his oppressed poor from under their "task-masters"; and it is enough for us to be used as instruments in the hand of God, in accomplishing his glorious purposes. (*Yes, yes.*)

Of so much importance do I consider the present position of the Liberty Party, in terminating the accursed system of slavery, from which I myself have been delivered, that I desire all its members may regard themselves as laborers, *under God*, in this great moral vineyard. His voice calls upon the dressers of that vineyard to bring to their aid all those means which lie in their power, whether moral or political, to remove the deadly evil from his heritage. To accomplish the object in view we must feel for the slaves "as bound with them," we must place ourselves, so far as we can, in their position, and go forward with the fixed consciousness that we are *free* or *enslaved* with them. (*Hear, hear.*)

It is maintained by many that we are to judge men by their complexion, and not by their moral worth. This spirit of *caste* the friends of freedom have trodden under foot; but it is not dead; it too often shows itself in our country, exerting a withering influence on those who cherish it, and chilling the heart's blood of those against whom it is exerted. But he who is considered so offensive for the complexion his Creator has given him, has the assurance that God "is no respecter of persons": and those who make this distinction are to be pitied for their ignorance of the works of God, and of the attributes of His character. It is amusing to see how this prejudice against color operates. You ask one of those color-haters, when he does not want your votes, if he is in favor of emancipation, and he says, "O no! it would destroy the country! I don't believe in your amalgamation!" But place the same political demagogue in view of the door of the Capitol, and he is quite another man: give him encouragement of political preferment, and he is—what is he not?—he is in favor of abolitionism, or any other ism that will enable him to accomplish his purpose!

It puts me in mind of the anecdote which is related of the Bishop of Rochester, who, before his preferment was in the most obscure circumstances, clad with the habiliments of poverty, and known by the name of John Delancey. The *Bishop* was loud in his denunciations of sin in all its forms, and often reproved those who used profane language, though he was known to have been formerly notorious for that sin. But his sacerdotal office did not entirely conceal his deformity of character, for he still indulged himself in *swearing in private.* One day he was heard by one of his parishioners taking God's holy name in vain; the man, of course, was confounded by his Bishop's profanity, and reproved him for it. The Bishop replied that he "did not swear as the Bishop of Rochester but as John Delancey." "But I would like to know," retorted the honest peasant, "what will become of the Bishop of Rochester when the Devil gets John Delancey! (*Hear*) The fact was, the Bishop of Rochester was the same man as John Delancey, his priestly robes could not conceal his wickedness or change his character. And that man who has "despised the day of small things" and heaped reproach on our cause, in the face of self evident truths, and in violation of the commands of God, can be very gracious and humane, now that the friends of Freedom are augmenting their forces and acquiring more and more energy at the ballot box. Such men, while clinging to the old pro-slavery parties would fain ride into power, on the backs of the time-worn, weather-beaten soldiers of abolition. But while they stand in their present position, they are not to be trusted with the guardianship of the rights of freemen; and whatever may be their professions, they are against us still.

The time is not far distant when the Liberty Party will be the most powerful party in our country; nothing can arrest its progress; our principles are sound, founded, as they are, upon eternal truth and justice, and

> That man is doubly armed,
> Who hath his quarrel just.

Efforts may indeed be made to oppose our onward course, but the mighty current of Anti-Slavery feeling will break through every barrier, like that "Father of Waters" which rolls its vast volume through the land of the Tyrant, increasing in power by being obstructed, till it overcomes all opposition, bearing on its surface or casting aside every obstacle, and moving onward with increasing velocity and grandeur to the bosom of the ocean. (*Applause*) What, sir, has the slave power done to oppose our progress? The voice of the sainted Lovejoy cries to us from the ground in tones of god-like power, to "*go forward*"; but did the spilling of his blood quench the holy fire of abolition in Alton? Did the destruction of Birney's press in Cincinnati prevent the spread of the startling facts and awful truths on the subject of slavery? No, sir, they only urge on the cause of freedom, and hasten the day of its final and glorious triumph.

But, sir, the Dark Spirit of Slavery hovers not only around Alton, but over our whole Union, from Maine to the Sabine, there are to be found men who bow in subserviency to the Slave Power. She is casting her huge shadow over our whole domain, and not content with her present limits, efforts are now making to enlarge her empire, and there is reason to fear that Texas, with its mass of abominations, *will be fastened upon the Union after all.*

But, sir, even this may be overruled to the destruction of the system. The North will not bear it. The mighty mass of slaves concentrated upon the extreme South will not bear it. Look at Eastern Virginia, with her soil worn out and good for nothing, by the effects of slavery, once rich and fertile as the Garden of Eden. See her now raising men, women and children to sell by the head and pound, in the New Orleans market; her citizens subsisting by the traffic of human flesh in violation of the Constitution of the United States, and bringing down upon our nation the righteous indignation of Heaven and the scorn of civilized man. Do you ask, were I there, trampled under foot by these traders in the souls of men, what I would do? I can't say precisely what I should do—but, sir, in the language of Shakespeare I will say, All that man dares do, I would do. (*Applause*)

Ah, sir, those heaving fires that formerly burst forth like the lava of a burning volcano, upon the inhabitants of Southampton and elsewhere, when the colored man rose and asserted *his rights to humanity and liberty,* are kept in check, only by the abolitionists. They hold open the safety valve of the nation;—and these *enemies of the country,* as they are called, are the very men, sir, that prevent a general insurrection of the slaves from spreading carnage and devastation throughout the entire South. They confide in the assurances of the abolitionists that something is doing to hasten the day when they "shall sit under their own vine and their own fig tree," and their claims to liberty and happiness be asserted and *established by Law.* Yes, sir. I repeat it,—the slaves *know* throughout the entire South, of the movement of the abolitionists, they know they have friends in the North in whom they may *confide* in case they are driven to desperation. (*True, true*)

But we are told—the slaves could not take care of themselves, if they were free." Not take care of themselves! when now they take care of themselves, and their masters too, and that under the blighting influence of slavery, with their energies crippled by its withering curse.

Take off from them the heavy chains under which they groan, and gratitude would spontaneously flow from every heart that now bleeds in slavery, gratitude to their benefactors, and loyalty to the government which had legislated in their behalf, while hope would "light up a smile," not "in the aspect of woe," but in prospect of possessing the fruits of their labor, their wives and their children, as was intended by their Creator, and their songs would rehearse the acts and glory of their deliverers down to the end of time. I cannot harbor the thought for a moment that their deliverance will be brought about by violence. No; our country will not be so deaf to the cries of the oppressed; so regardless of the commands of God, and her highest interests. No, the time for a last stern struggle has not yet come (may it never be necessary.) The finger of the Almighty will hold back the trigger, and his all powerful arm will sheathe the sword till the oppressor's cup is full. (*Hear, hear*)

The slaveholders count upon numbers; we upon *truth*, and it "is powerful and will prevail." Whoever will read the Declaration of Independence carefully, will be convinced that it is on our side, the textbook of our party—setting forth, as it does, "that all men are created equal," what is the inference to be drawn from it in regard to the slaves? Why that they all are *to do just as other men do.* It asserts that "*all men*" are entitled to "life, liberty, and the pursuit of happiness." Not this man here, and that man there, but "*all men*" are equally entitled to the inalienable rights and privileges with which they are endowed by their Creator. Such language as is embodied in the Declaration of Independence would lead the framers of it, were they now living, to fight in our cause.

Is it said that it is folly to pass these resolutions, and

take such a position as is occupied by the Liberty Party? There are, I know, professed abolitionists, who say that we can never accomplish our object, and who prophesy our overthrow. To them I would say, that, standing on the rock of principle, no weapon of the enemy can prevail against us; and in conclusion I would remind them of the anecdote of an honest man from Dublin, who while laying the foundation of a wall was laughed at by his neighbors. "You may build your wall," said they, "five feet high, and four feet broad, and when Jack Frost comes, he will throw it over." "Oh, then," retorted the builder, "I will make it four feet high, and five feet broad, and then if Jack overturns it, *it will be a foot higher than ever.*" (*Laughter and applause*)

4.

AN ADDRESS TO THE SLAVES OF THE UNITED STATES OF AMERICA, BUFFALO, N.Y., 1843

Brethren and Fellow-Citizens:—Your brethren of the North, East, and West have been accustomed to meet together in National Conventions, to sympathize with each other, and to weep over your unhappy condition. In these meetings we have addressed all classes of the free, but we have never, until this time, sent a word of consolation and advice to you. We have been contented in sitting still and mourning over your sorrows, earnestly hoping that before this day your sacred liberties would have been restored. But, we have hoped in vain. Years have rolled on, and tens of thousands have been borne on streams of blood and tears, to the shores of eternity. While you have been oppressed, we have also been partakers with you; nor can we be free while you are enslaved. We, therefore, write to you as being bound with you.

Many of you are bound to us, not only by the ties of a common humanity, but we are connected by the more tender relations of parents, wives, husbands, children, brothers, and sisters, and friends. As such we most affectionately address you.

Slavery has fixed a deep gulf between you and us, and while it shuts out from you the relief and consolation which your friends would willingly render, it afflicts and persecutes you with a fierceness which we might not expect to see in the fiends of hell. But still the Almighty Father of mercies has left to us a glimmering ray of hope, which shines out like a lone star in a cloudy sky. Mankind are becoming wiser, and better—the oppressor's power is fading, and you, every day, are becoming better informed, and more numerous. Your grievances, brethren, are many. We shall not attempt, in this short address, to present to the world all the dark catalogue of this nation's sins, which have been committed upon an innocent people. Nor is it indeed necessary, for you feel them from day to day, and all the civilized world look upon them with amazement.

Two hundred and twenty-seven years ago, the first of our injured race were brought to the shores of America. They came not with glad spirits to select their homes in the New World. They came not with their own consent, to find an unmolested enjoyment of the blessings of this fruitful soil. The first dealings they had with men calling themselves Christians, exhibited to them the worst features of corrupt and sordid hearts: and convinced them that no cruelty is too great, no villainy and no robbery too abhorrent for even enlightened men to perform, when influenced by avarice and lust. Neither did they come flying upon the wings of Liberty, to a land of freedom. But they came with broken hearts, from their beloved native land, and were doomed to unrequited toil and deep degradation. Nor did the evil of their bondage end at their emancipation by death. Succeeding generations inherited their chains, and millions have come from eternity into time, and have returned again to the world of spirits, cursed and ruined by American slavery.

The propagators of the system, or their immediate ancestors, very soon discovered its growing evil, and its tre-mendous wickedness, and secret promises were made to destroy it. The gross inconsistency of a people holding slaves, who had themselves "ferried o'er the wave" for freedom's sake, was too apparent to be entirely overlooked. The voice of Freedom cried, "Emancipate your slaves." Humanity supplicated with tears for the deliverance of the children of Africa. Wisdom urged her solemn plea. The bleeding captive pleaded his innocence, and pointed to Christianity who stood weeping at the cross. Jehovah frowned upon the nefarious institution, and thunderbolts, red with vengeance, struggled to leap forth to blast the guilty wretches who maintained it. But all was vain. Slavery had stretched its dark wings of death over the land, the Church stood silently by—the priests prophesied falsely, and the people loved to have it so. Its throne is established, and now it reigns triumphant.

Nearly three millions of your fellow-citizens are prohib-ited by law and public opinion (which in this country is stronger than law) from reading the Book of Life. Your intellect has been destroyed as much as possible, and every ray of light they have attempted to shut cut from your minds. The oppressors themselves have become in-volved in the ruin. They have become weak, sensual, and rapacious—they have cursed you—they have cursed them-selves—they have cursed the earth which they have trod.

The colonists threw the blame upon England. They said that the mother country entailed the evil upon them, and that they would rid themselves of it if they could. The world thought they were sincere, and the philanthropic pitied them. But time soon tested their sincerity. In a few years the colonists grew strong, and severed themselves from the British Government. Their independence was declared, and they took their station among the sovereign powers of the earth. The declaration was a glorious docu-ment. Sages admired it, and the patriotic of every nation reverenced the God-like sentiments which it contained. When the power of Government returned to their hands, did they emancipate the slaves? No; they rather added new links to our chains. Were they ignorant of the principles of Liberty? Certainly they were not. The sentiments of their revolutionary orators fell in burning eloquence upon their hearts, and with one voice they cried, *Liberty or Death*. Oh what a sentence was that! It ran from soul to soul like electric fire, and nerved the arm of thousands to fight in the holy cause of Freedom. Among the diversity of opinions that are entertained in regard to physical resistance, there are but a few found to gainsay that stern declaration. We are among those who do not.

Slavery! How much misery is comprehended in that single word. What mind is there that does not shrink from its direful effects? Unless the image of God be obliterated from the soul, all men cherish the love of Liberty. The nice discerning political economist does not regard the sacred right more than the untutored African who roams in the wilds of Congo. Nor has the one more right to the full enjoyment of his freedom than the other. In every man's mind the good seeds of liberty are planted, and he who brings his fellow down so low, as to make him contented with a condition of slavery, commits the highest crime against God and man. Brethren, your oppressors aim to do this. They endeavor to make you as much like brutes as possible. When they have blinded the eyes of your mind—when they have embittered the sweet waters of life—when they have shut out the light which shines from the word of God—then, and not till then, has American slavery done its perfect work.

To such Degradation it is sinful in the Extreme for you to make voluntary Submission. The divine commandments you are in duty bound to reverence and obey. If you do not obey them, you will surely meet with the displeasure of the Almighty. He requires you to love him supremely, and your neighbor as yourself—to keep the Sabbath day holy— to search the Scriptures—and bring up your children with respect for his laws, and to worship no other God but him. But slavery sets all these at nought, and hurls defiance in the face of Jehovah. The forlorn condition in which you are placed, does not destroy your moral obligation to God. You are not certain of heaven, because you suffer yourselves to remain in a state of slavery, where you cannot obey the commandments of the Sovereign of the universe. If the ignorance of slavery is a passport to heaven, then it is a blessing, and no curse, and you should rather desire its perpetuity than its abolition. God will not receive slavery, nor ignorance, nor any other state of mind, for love and obedience to him. Your condition does not absolve you from your moral obligation. The diabolical injustice by which your liberties are cloven down, *neither God, nor angels, or just men, command you to suffer for a single moment. Therefore it is your solemn and imperative duty to use every means, both moral, intellectual, and physical, that promises success.* If a band of heathen men should attempt to enslave a race of Christians, and to place their children under the influence of some false religion, surely, Heaven would frown upon the men who would not resist such aggression, even to death. If, on the other hand, a band of Christians should attempt to enslave a race of heathen men, and to entail slavery upon them, and to keep them in heathenism in the midst of Christianity, the God of heaven would smile upon every effort which the injured might make to disenthral themselves.

Brethren, it is as wrong for your lordly oppressors to keep you in slavery, as it was for the man thief to steal our ancestors from the coast of Africa. You should therefore now use the same manner of resistance, as would have been just in our ancestors, when the bloody footprints of the first remorseless soul-thief was placed upon the shores of our fatherland. The humblest peasant is as free in the sight of God as the proudest monarch that ever swayed a sceptre. Liberty is a spirit sent out from God, and like its great Author, is no respecter of persons.

Brethren, the time has come when you must act for yourselves. It is an old and true saying that, "if hereditary bondmen would be free, they must themselves strike the blow." You can plead your own cause, and do the work of emancipation better than any others. The nations of the old world are moving in the great cause of universal freedom, and some of them at least will, ere long, do you justice. The combined powers of Europe have placed their broad seal of disapprobation upon the African slave-trade. But in the slave-holding parts of the United States, the trade is as brisk as ever. They buy and sell you as though you were brute beasts. The North has done much —her opinion of slavery in the abstract is known. But in regard to the South, we adopt the opinion of the *New York Evangelist*—"We have advanced so far, that the cause apparently waits for a more effectual door to be thrown open than has been yet." We are about to point you to that more effectual door. Look around you, and behold the bosoms of your loving wives heaving with untold agonies! Hear the cries of your poor children! Remember the stripes your fathers bore. Think of the torture and disgrace of your noble mothers. Think of your wretched sisters, loving virtue and purity, as they are driven into concubinage and are exposed to the unbridled lusts of incarnate devils. Think of the undying glory that hangs around the ancient name of Africa:—and forget not that you are native-born American citizens, and as such, you are justly entitled to all the rights that are granted to the freest. Think how many tears you have poured out upon the soil which you have cultivated with unrequited toil and enriched with your blood; and then go to your lordly enslavers and tell them plainly, that you *are determined to be free*. Appeal to their sense of justice, and tell them that they have no more right to oppress you, than you have to enslave them. Entreat them to remove the grievous burdens which they have imposed upon you, and to remunerate you for your labor. Promise them renewed diligence in the cultivation of the soil, if they will render to you an equivalent for your services. Point them to the increase of happiness and prosperity in the British West-Indies since the Act of Emancipation. Tell them in language which they cannot misunderstand, of the exceeding sinfulness of slavery, and of a future judgment, and of the righteous retributions of an indignant God. Inform them that all you desire is *freedom*, and that nothing else will suffice. Do this, and for ever after cease to toil for the heartless tyrants, who give you no other reward but stripes and abuse. If they then commence the work of death, they, and not you, will be responsible for the consequences. You had far better all die—*die immediately*, than live slaves, and entail your wretchedness upon your posterity. If you would be free in this generation, here is your only hope. However much you and all of us may desire it, there is not much hope of redemption without the shedding of blood. If you must bleed, let it all come at once—rather *die freemen, than live to be the slaves*. It is impossible, like the children of Israel, to make a grand exodus from the land of bondage. The Pharaohs are on both sides of the blood-red waters! You cannot move *en masse*, to the dominions of the British Queen—nor can you pass through Florida and overrun Texas, and at last find peace in Mexico. The propagators of American slavery are spending their blood and treasure, that they may plant the black flag in the heart of Mexico and riot in the halls of the Montezumas. In the language of the Rev. Robert Hall, when addressing the volunteers of Bristol, who were rushing forth to repel the invasion of Napoleon, who threatened to lay waste the fair homes of England, "Religion is too much interested in your behalf, not to shed over you her most gracious influences."

You will not be compelled to spend much time in order to become inured to hardships. From the first moment that you breathed the air of heaven, you have been accustomed to nothing else but hardships. The heroes of the American Revolution were never put upon harder fare than a peck of corn and a few herrings per week. You have not become enervated by the luxuries of life. Your sternest energies have been beaten out upon the anvil of severe trial. Slavery has done this, to make you subservient to its own purposes;

but it has done more than this, it has prepared you for any emergency. If you receive good treatment, it is what you could hardly expect; if you meet with pain, sorrow, and even death, these are the common lot of the slaves.

Fellow-men! patient sufferers! behold your dearest rights crushed to the earth! See your sons murdered, and your wives, mothers and sisters doomed to prostitution. In the name of the merciful God, and by all that life is worth, let it no longer be a debatable question, whether it is better to choose *Liberty* or *death*.

In 1822, Denmark Veazie, of South Carolina, formed a plan for the liberation of his fellow-men. In the whole history of human efforts to overthrow slavery, a more complicated and tremendous plan was never formed. He was betrayed by the treachery of his own people, and died a martyr to freedom. Many a brave hero fell, but history, faithful to her high trust, will transcribe his name on the same monument with Moses, Hampden, Tell, Bruce and Wallace, Toussaint L'Ouverture, Lafayette and Washington. That tremendous movement shook the whole empire of slavery. The guilty soul-thieves were overwhelmed with fear. It is a matter of fact, that at that time, and in consequence of the threatened revolution, the slave States talked strongly of emancipation. But they blew but one blast of the trumpet of freedom, and then laid it aside. As these men became quiet, the slaveholders ceased to talk about emancipation: and now behold your condition today! Angels sigh over it, and humanity has long since exhausted her tears in weeping on your account!

The patriotic Nathaniel Turner followed Denmark Veazie. He was goaded to desperation by wrong and injustice. By despotism, his name has been recorded on the list of infamy, and future generations will remember him among the noble and brave.

Next arose the immortal Joseph Cinque, the hero of the *Amistad.* He was a native African, and by the help of God he emancipated a whole ship-load of his fellow-men on the high seas. And he now sings of liberty on the sunny hills of Africa and beneath his native palm-trees, where he hears the lion roar and feels himself as free as that king of the forest.

Next arose Madison Washington, that bright star of freedom, and took his station in the constellation of true heroism. He was a slave on board the brig *Creole*, of Richmond, bound to New Orleans, that great slave mart, with a hundred and four others. Nineteen struck for liberty or death. But one life was taken, and the whole were emancipated, and the vessel was carried into Nassau, New Providence.

Noble men! Those who have fallen in freedom's conflict, their memories will be cherished by the true-hearted and the God-fearing in all future generations; those who are living, their names are surrounded by a halo of glory.

Brethren, arise, arise! Strike for your lives and liberties. Now is the day and the hour. Let every slave throughout the land do this, and the days of slavery are numbered. You cannot be more oppressed than you have been—you cannot suffer greater cruelties than you have already. *Rather die freemen than live to be slaves.* Remember that you are *four millions!*

It is in your power so to torment the God-cursed slaveholders, that they will be glad to let you go free. If the scale was turned, and black men were the masters and white men the slaves, every destructive agent and element would be employed to lay the oppressor low. Danger and death would hang over their heads day and night. Yes, the tyrants would meet with plagues more terrible than those of Pharaoh. But you are a patient people. You act as though you were made for the special use of these devils. You act as though your daughters were born to pamper the lusts of your masters and overseers. And worse than all, you tamely submit while your lords tear your wives from your embraces and defile them before your eyes. In the name of God, we ask, are you men? Where is the blood of your fathers? Has it all run out of your veins? Awake, awake; millions of voices are calling you! Your dead fathers speak to you from their graves. Heaven, as with a voice of thunder, calls on you to arise from the dust.

Let your motto be resistance! *resistance! resistance!* No oppressed people have ever secured their liberty without resistance. What kind of resistance you had better make, you must decide by the circumstances that surround you, and according to the suggestion of expediency. Brethren, adieu! Trust in the living God. Labor for the peace of the human race, and remember that you are *four millions.*

5.

LETTER TO MRS. MARIA W. CHAPMAN, NOVEMBER 17, 1843

Respected Madam:

Some time ago you wrote an article in the *Liberator,* condemnatory of the National Convention of colored people, which was held in the city of Buffalo, in the month of August last. I should have sent a reply, ere this time, had I not been engaged so much in the cause of freedom, since the appearance of your article. I must confess that I was exceedingly amazed to find that I was doomed to share so much of your severity, to call it nothing else. And, up to this moment, I have not been able to understand the motives which led you to attack my character as you have in the paper referred to. I am a stranger to you, comparatively, and whatever of my public life has come to your notice, you have seen nothing impeachable. I was born in slavery, and have escaped, to tell you, and others, what the monster has done, and is still doing. It, therefore, astonished me to think that you should desire to sink me again to the condition of a *slave,* by forcing me to think just as you do. My crime is, that I have dared to think, and act, contrary to your opinion. I am a Liberty party man— you are opposed to that party—far be it from me to attempt to injure your character because you cannot pronounce my shibboleth. While you think as you do, we must

differ. If it has come to this, that I must think and act as
you do, because you are an abolitionist, or be exterminated
by your thunder, then I do not hesitate to say that your
abolitionism is abject slavery. Were I a slave of the Hon.
George McDuffie, or John C. Calhoun, I would not be required to do anything more than to think and act as I
might be commanded. I will not be the slave of any person
or party. I am a Liberty party man from choice. No man
ever asked me to join that party; I was the first colored
man that ever attached his name to that party, and you
may rely upon my word, when I tell you I mean "to stand."

You likewise adopt all that E. M. Marsh, of Buffalo, has
said of the Convention and myself. I shall not attempt to
say anything more than this, in regard to him. My friend,
Mr. March, is a man of a very unstable mind. He is one
thing to-day, and another thing to-morrow. He was once a
Liberty man, but he is now a no-church and no-govern-
ment man. I never saw such an unfair statement penned
by a man calling himself a Christian. Every thing that he
has written, is either false, or exaggerated. I have no more
to say of him—I leave him alone in his glory. But I am
sorry that you have echoed his false allegations. I am sorry
that all the old organization journals have likewise echoed
that libellous report.

But the address to the slaves you seem to doom to the
most fiery trials. And yet, madam, you have not seen that
address—you have merely *heard* of it; nevertheless, you
criticised it very severely. You speak, at length, of myself,
the author of the paper. You say that I "have received bad
counsel." You are not the only person who has told your
humble servant that his humble productions have been
produced by the *"counsel"* of some anglo-saxon. I have
expected no more from ignorant slaveholders and their
apologists, but I really looked for better things from Mrs.
Maria W. Chapman, an anti-slavery poetess, and editor
pro tem. of the Boston *Liberator*. I can think on the subject
of human rights without "counsel," either from the men of
the West, or the women of the East. My address was read

to but two persons, previous to its presentation at Buffalo. One was a colored brother, who did not give me a single word of counsel, and the other was my wife; and if she did counsel me, it is no matter, for "we twain are one flesh." In a few days I hope to publish the address, then you can judge how much treason there is in it. In the mean time, be assured that there is one black American who dares to speak boldly on the subject of universal liberty.

I am, very respectfully,
Your servant,
Henry Highland Garnet

25, Liberty-street, Troy, N. Y.

6.

LETTER TO L. A. CHOMEROW ON JAMAICAN SOCIETY, OCTOBER 2, 1854

My dear sir,

I am in the receipt of your circular dated July, 1854, which came to hand some four weeks ago, and I take this occasion to answer the several questions which are contained in it, sofar as I am able. (1) The physical condition of the laboring classes in Jamaica is not inferior to that of any other people with whom I have met moving in the same sphere of life and with their limited amount of education. Consequently their limited ideas of the comforts and wants of life are taken into account. Their condition is much better than one would naturally expect to see. The present rising generation are physically a fine healthy race of people. (2) They are a temperate people and when it is borne in mind that rum-making is one of their most common employments, I can safely say that their general sobriety is astonishing. They are orderly and law-abiding, and in the rural districts they require less physical force for their government than is necessary for the same class of people in England and Ireland. When compared with the same class in Europe and in America they are not equal to the inhabitants of these countries in industry. But if compared with people of other tropical regions they are not behind them in this respect. The duties of religion are sadly neglected by many, and I may say by the great majority; notwithstanding, there are many faithful witnesses for the truth among them. I have sometimes thought that perhaps too much is expected from them in matters of religion. We ought to take the divine view of their case— where little is given little is required. The curses of the worst examples which have been before them and their ancestors for centuries are still resting upon them. The majority of those who are their superiors as regards their positions in society, are not their superiors in morality. To speak plainly, the habits of too many of the whites are wicked, disgusting, and bestial. Many of them are anxious to educate their children; this desire, however, is not the same in every district. There are fine schools in our districts, embracing a circuit of ten or fifteen miles. Three belong to this church of which I am the minister, having about 200 pupils, and are under my superintendence. One belongs to the Church of England, and one to the Baptists. All of them are open to the people without the least denominational distinction. (3) Much of the labour in this district is performed upon the sugar estates by females, quite as many as there are men. This same remark is also true of the mountain districts where nearly all the provisions are raised. In this part of the island there are not as many children twelve or fifteen years of age employed in the field except at crop time. (4) Agricultural work is most generally given out by jobs, otherwise they receive from sixpence to one shilling and sixpence per day. Carpenters and masons receive from two shillings to three shillings and sixpence. All classes of labourers might earn more if they would but economize their time. Field labourers commence work at 6 or 7 o'clock A.M. and where jobs are taken they frequently cease at 11 o'clock. At 4 P.M. all kinds of labourers draw off. (5) They do not consider their wages to be sufficient and just and this fact furnishes the principal ground upon which the people refuse to do more work. There is no such thing as a change in wages. The planter fixes the amount and he is the sole judge and arbiter in the matter—and the almost universal opinion of the planters is that to give the people more wages would be tempting them to do less work. The working people, in their turn, affirm that at the present low rate of wages they can do better to cultivate their provision grounds, which with less labour will yield them a better return. This last popular observation is true, and will remain so, as long as there are a sufficient number of people on the estates who make cash enough to purchase their provisions. This unphilosophical mode of procedure may be satisfactory to both classes for a season, but a crisis must ultimately arrive which will prove disastrous to both. It is an undeniable fact that those who work five days in the week on the estates receive barely sufficient [wages] for market purchases on Saturday, while the small cultivation of provisions works half that time and obtains the same with comparative ease. (6) Many of them desire to become freeholders, and a goodly number have become such, but it is very difficult for them to get good land by purchase. Large landed proprietors do not in the least encourage them in this respect and they scarcely ever sell to them unless they are compelled to do so by necessity. Even the thrown up estates are usually bought entirely by some capitalist who is willing to sell only as he purchased—that is entirely. To this statement, there are some rare exceptions. Most of the villages which have sprung up since emancipation have been purchased by missionaries and other philanthropists and sold out to the people on lots to suit their convenience. This was the case with the village of Stirling in which I reside—it was bought up by one of my predecessors, the Reverend William Niven, and sold to an industrious class of people. The planters generally believe that to encourage them to become landowners would place them in a position of independence, and they are not encouraged in their efforts to become owners of the soil. If they buy land it is generally that which is the poorest, and not [that] which is valuable to the planters. A few days ago I was speaking to an educated and highly respectable proprietor of large estates, respecting the cultivation of fibrous plants by the peasantry of the country and the desirableness of their getting good land for that purpose. He simply replied, "When you speak of their getting good land you speak of an impossibility." I asked him, "How could this be an impossibility?" "Because," said he, "such land is not to be bought by them." But thanks be to God he has so bountifully scattered his blessings over the island, that even the poor soil is productive. In the single parish of Manchester, which is a mountain region, the merchants of Kingston are said to have paid to the inhabitants thereof for their coffee and pimento during this last year, the handsome sum of thirty thousand pounds sterling —and that most of these staple productions were raised by small landholders. (7) Many are cultivating canes upon their grounds and they readily dispose of their sugars at the markets for double the price which the same qualities could bring in the English markets. Any inferior sugar here is sold in the market for sixpence per pound. But this department of enterprise among the labouring people is also looked upon with jealousy by the planters, and is discouraged. Those who raise their own canes in the vicinity of estates usually grind and boil their crops, as the estate's proprietors, which they are freely allowed to do for the sake of the "drippings" which are valuable in rum-making. A black neighbor of mine has a considerable cane field and he and a friend of his are about to put up a small boiling house and a still. But the proprietor of the estate to which the poor man's lot was contiguously situated heard of the arrangement and rode into the yard of the enterprising black and the following conversation and results took place: "So you are going to turn planter." "How so master?"

"Why I hear that you are going to grind your canes, and boil your sugar." "Yes master I was intending to do so." "Well I should not like to see you doing anything of the kind. You must remember that you have no title to the land you occupy and I doubt you will ever get one if you persist in your undertaking." I am informed that the poor man had been completely overawed by the threat, and will proceed no further. The only reasons that can be assigned for this unjustifiable and tyrannical conduct are that the planter fears that he might lose some of his canes, and that this example might be the means of inducing others to venture the same enterprise. (8) They rent their grounds on equitable terms but at the same time they stipulate the full value for them. Some people in this vicinity pay 20 shillings a year for their provision grounds, others pay less, and sometimes they use the lands without the knowledge or permission of the owners. (9) They are quite willing to work for masters who treat them kindly and discreetly. (10) Many of the planters treat them with civility—and many exhibit an opposite feeling toward them. They are not often treated with personal violence for they are quite willing to defend themselves by law or otherwise. (11) Prejudice against colour is marked and strong, and exists more or less in the social institutions of the land. But as the laws are just and equal, all men can alike make their way to distinction and this they are achieving. (12) There is less immorality in country places than there is in the towns. (13) The natives look with suspicion on immigration as is now carried on in Jamaica. (14) Coloured people are found in every department of civil government. The police is entirely composed of that class of our citizens. (15) Many of them have increased their property. In conclusion, I would say that it is becoming more and more apparent that the emancipated people use their liberty with more moderation and propriety than their former masters exercise government over them. It is also a fact which ought by no means to be forgotten that if the former slaveholders are sinking, the emancipated are rising daily.

I am dear sir, yours truly,
Henry Highland Garnet

L. A. Chomerow, Esq.

7.

THE PAST AND THE PRESENT CONDITION AND THE DESTINY OF THE COLORED RACE, TROY, 1848

Ladies and Gentlemen:

My theme is the Past and the Present condition, and the Destiny of the Colored race. The path of thought which you are invited to travel, has not as I am aware, been pursued heretofore to any considerable extent. The Present, is the midway between the Past and the Future. Let us ascend that sublime eminence, that we may view the vast empire of ruin that is scarcely discernible through the mists of former ages; and if, while we are dwelling upon the desolations that meet our eyes, we shall mourn over them, I entreat you to look upward and behold the bright scenery of the future. There we have a clear sky, and from thence are refreshing breezes. The airy plains are radiant with prophetic brightness, and truth, love, and liberty are descending the heavens, bearing the charter of man's destiny to a waiting world.

All the various forms of truth that are presented to the minds of men, are in perfect harmony with the government of God. Many things that appear to be discordant are not really so; for when they are understood, and the mind becomes illuminated and informed, the imagined deformities disappear as spectres depart from the vision of one who has been a maniac, when his reason returns. "God is the rock, his work is perfect—a God of truth, and without iniquity. Justice and judgment are the habitations of his throne, and mercy and truth go before his face. His righteousness is an everlasting righteousness, and his law is the truth."

The truth will profit us nothing if we suffer it not to clothe us in our right minds—it returns without accomplishing its high mission to us, if we refuse to let her lead us to the delectable mountain, from whence we can behold the pure stream of the law of Jehovah, flowing from his throne, hailed by angel voices and the music of the spheres.

In order to pursue my subject I must, for the sake of distinction, use some of the improper terms of our times. I shall, therefore, speak of *races*, when in fact there is but one race, as there was but one Adam.

By an almost common consent, the modern world seems determined to pilfer Africa of her glory. It were not enough that her children have been scattered over the globe, clothed in the garments of shame—humiliated and oppressed—but her merciless foes weary themselves in plundering the tombs of our renowned sires, and in obliterating their worthy deeds, which were inscribed by fame upon the pages of ancient history.

The three grand divisions of the earth that were known to the ancients, were colonized by the three sons of Noah. Shem was the father of the Asiatics—the Africans descended from Ham, and Japheth was the progenitor of the Europeans. These men being the children of one father, they were originally of the same complexion—for we cannot through the medium of any law of nature or reason, come to the conclusion, that one was black, another was copper-colored, and the other was white. Adam was a red man, and by what law of nature his descendants became dissimilar to him, is a problem which is yet to be clearly solved. The fact that the universal Father has varied the complexions of his children, does not detract from his mercy, or give us reason to question his wisdom.

Moses is the patriarch of sacred history. The same eminent station is occupied by Herodotus in profane history. To the chronicles of these two great men we are indebted for all the information we have in relation to the early condition of man. If they are incorrect, to what higher authority shall we appeal—and if they are true, then we may acquaint ourselves with the history of our race from that period,

When yonder spheres sublime,
Peal'd their first notes to sound the march of time.

Ham was the first African. Egypt was settled by an immediate descendant of Ham, who, in sacred history, is called Mesraim, and in uninspired history he is known by the name of Menes. Yet in the face of this historical evidence, there are those who affirm that the ancient Egyptians were not of the pure African stock. The gigantic statue of the Sphinx has the peculiar features of the children of Ham—one of the most celebrated queens of Egypt was Nitocris, an Ethiopian woman; yet these intellectual resurrectionists dig through a mountain of such evidence, and declare that these people were not negroes.

We learn from Herodotus, that the ancient Egyptians were black, and had woolly hair. These people astonished the world with their arts and sciences, in which they revelled with unbounded prodigality. They became the masters of the East, and the lords of the Hebrews. No arm less powerful than Jehovah's, could pluck the children of Abraham from their hands. The plagues were marshalled against them, and the pillars of cloud and of fire, and at last the resistless sea. "Then the horse and the rider, sank like lead in the mighty waters." But the kingdom of the Ptolemys was still great. The most exalted mortal eulogium that could be spoken of Moses, was that he was learned in all the learning of the Egyptians. It was from them that he gathered the materials with which he reared that grand superstructure, partaking of law, poetry, and history, which has filled the world with wonder and praise. Mournful reverses of fortune have passed over that illustrious people. The star that arose in such matchless splendor above the eastern horizon has had its setting. But Egypt, Africa's dark browed queen, still lives. Her pyramid tombs—her sculptured columns dug from the sands to adorn modern architecture—the remnants of her once impregnable walls —the remains of her hundred gated city, rising over the wide-spread ruins, as if to guard the fame of the race that gave them existence, all proclaim what she once was.

Whatever may be the extent of prejudice against color, as it is falsely called, and is so generally practiced in this country, Solomon, the most renowned of kings, possessed none of it. Among the seven hundred wives, and the three hundred concubines, who filled his houses, the most favored queen was a beautiful sable daughter of one of the Pharaohs of Egypt. In order to take her to his bosom, he trampled upon the laws of his nation, and incurred the divine displeasure—for a Jew might not espouse any heathen or idolater who was not circumcised in heart. When he had secured her, he bowed his great intellect before her, that he might do her that homage which he paid to no other woman. Solomon was a poet, and pure love awakened the sweetest melody in his soul. To her honor and praise he composed that beautiful poem called the Canticles, or Solomon's Song. For her he wove that gorgeous wreath which is unsurpassed in its kind, and with his own royal hand placed it upon her dark brow. Several persons are represented in the poem, and it is composed of an interesting colloquy. The reader is introduced to "the watchmen that went about the streets," and to "the daughters of Jerusalem," and to the bride and the groom, which are the king and the beauteous Egyptian. It is not at all surprising that she who received such distinguished marks of kingly favors, should encounter the jealousy of the daughters of Jerusalem. They saw that the Egyptian woman had monopolised the heart of the son of David, and the royal poet represents his queen to say to her fairer but supplanted rivals:—

I am black but comely,
O ye daughters of Jerusalem,
As the tents of Kedar,
As the curtains of Solomon.
Look not upon me, because I am black,
Because the sun has looked upon me.

Thus she speaks of the superiority which nature had given her over the women of Jerusalem. She was handsome, and like all handsome women, she knew it.

The bride again speaks, and says to the bride-groom:—

I have compared thee, O my love,
To a company of horses in Pharaoh's chariot.

How inappropriate were this allusion if it had been placed in the mouth of any one else but an Egyptian. To give the passage any other interpretation is virtually accusing Solomon of grosser ignorance than my reverence will allow me to attribute to him.

Professor Stowe and President Mahan, and others, agree in giving the following translation to another verse in the first chapter of the song,

Ere I was aware
My soul was as the war-chariot
Of my noble people.

The whole poem, without doubt, is nothing more than a brilliant out-burst of Solomon's love for his bride.

Homer, the prince of epic poets, speaks of the Ethiopians, and presents them at the feast of the gods. These men of sun-burnt faces, as their name implies, he calls the excellent Ethiopians.

A distinguished scholar,* speaking of this passage in the Grecian's renowned poem, in the presence of an American pedant, the young upstart seriously inquired

* Rev. Beriah Green.

if the Ethiopians were black. "Most assuredly," answered
the scholar. "Well," said the young republican, "had I been
at that feast, and negroes had been placed at the table, I
would have left it." "Had you been living at that time,"
returned the other, "you would have been saved the trouble
of leaving the table, for the gods would not have invited
you."

Such a man in such a banquet would have been as much
out of place as an ass would be in a concert of sacred
music.

The interior of Ethiopia has not been explored by
modern adventurers. The antiquarian has made his way
into almost every dominion where relics of former greatness have promised to reward him for his toil. But this
country, as though she had concealed some precious
treasure, meets the traveller on the outskirts of her dominions, with pestilence and death. Yet, in the Highlands
which have been traversed, many unequivocal traces of
former civilization have been discovered. Very lately,
British enterprise has made some important researches in
that region of country, all of which go to prove that
Homer did not misplace his regards for them, when he
associated them with the gods.

The wife of Moses was an Ethiopian woman, and when
Miriam, his sister, murmured against her, the Almighty
smote Miriam, and she became white. Whether the mur-
muring arose on account of the complexion of the great
Lawgiver's wife, or from some other cause, I will not
attempt to determine. Whatever was the cause, we all
see how Jehovah regarded it, how fierce was his indignation, and how terrible his punishment. He came down
and stood in a cloudy pillar, and cursed the woman in
whose bosom the unholy prejudice was harbored.*

Ethiopia is one of the few nations whose destiny is
spoken of in prophecy. This is done in language so plain
that we are not driven to dubious inferences.

It is said that "Princes shall come out of Egypt, and

* Numbers, 12 chap. 10 v.

Ethiopia shall soon stretch out her hands unto God." It is thought by some that this divine declaration was fulfilled when Philip baptised the converted eunuch of the household of Candes, the Queen of the Ethiopians. In this transaction, a part of the prophecy may have been fulfilled, and only a part.

A vision seen by another prophet has become a matter of history. Hosea, foresaw that God would call his son out of Egypt, and when the infant Redeemer could find no shelter in the land of the Hebrews, he found an asylum in Egypt, where he remained until Herod was dead. He then returned to his native country, and in that event he fulfilled the declaration of the holy seer.

Numerous other instances might be mentioned that would indicate the ancient fame of our ancestors. A fame, which arose from every virtue, and talent, that render mortals pre-eminently great. From the conquests of love and beauty, from the prowess of their arms, and their architecture, poetry, mathematics, generosity, and piety. I will barely allude to the beautiful Cleopatra, who swayed and captivated the heart of Antony. To Hannibal, the sworn enemy and the scourge of Rome—the mighty General who crossed the Alps to meet his foes—the Alps which had never before been crossed by an army, nor never since, if we except Napoleon, the ambitious Corsican. To Terence, Euclid, Cyprian, Origen, and Augustine.

At this time, when these representatives of our race were filling the world with amazement, the ancestors of the now proud and boasting Anglo Saxons were among the most degraded of the human family. They abode in caves under ground, either naked or covered with the skins of wild beasts. Night was made hideous by their wild shouts, and day was darkened by the smoke which arose from bloody altars, upon which they offered human sacrifice.

For a long series of years, immediately following her brilliant era, the history of Africa appears not to be animated by many stirring events. Somewhere about the year of 1511, Charles V, of Spain, procured slaves from the

coast of Guinea, and sent them to Hispaniola. Bartholo-
mew Las Casas, a Roman Catholic priest, and afterwards
Bishop Chioppa, came to this new world, which had just
been called out of obscurity by the adventurous spirit of
Christopher Columbus. He left Spain under the auspices
of Charles. The Castilian Monarch had enslaved the Indians who inhabited his dominions, but soon found that
they were unprofitable in such a relation. Encouraged by
his Clerical confidant, his evil genius, he introduced into
South America a number of slaves from Africa, because
one black man could do as much labor as four Indians.
Las Casas, in mercy to the aborigines, recommended to
Cardinal Zimcrnes, to enslave the children of Africa. The
Cardinal, to his honor be it said, objected to the project,
but nevertheless the trade went on. The number was at
first limited at four thousand, but as might be expected
this numerical boundary was soon over-stepped. A trade
that was found to be so lucrative, was ultimately taken
up by almost every Christian nation, until that unhappy
country was annually plundered of 300,000 of her children. Future generations will gaze upon the names of the
guilty priest and King, in that contemptuous position
where they have placed themselves. Shame will deepen
the hatred of their memory, as men become enlightened
and just, and clouds of infamy will thicken around them
as the world moves on towards God.

In 1620, the very same year in which the Pilgrims
landed on the cold and rocky shores of New England, a
Dutch ship freighted with souls touched the banks of
James River, where the wretched people were employed as
slaves in the cultivation of that hateful weed, tobacco.
Wonderful coincidence! The angel of liberty hovered over
New England, and the Demon of slavery unfurled his
black flag over the fields of the "sunny south."

But latterly the slave-trade has been pronounced to be
piracy by most all of the civilized world. Great Britain has
discarded the chattel principle throughout her dominions.
In 1824 Mexico proclaimed freedom to her slaves. The

Pope of Rome, and the sovereigns of Turkey, and Denmark, and other nations bow at the shrine of Liberty. But France has laid the richest offering upon the altar of freedom, that has been presented to God in these latter days. In achieving her almost bloodless revolution, she maintained an admirable degree of consistency. The same blast of the trumpet of Liberty that rang through the halls of the Tuileries, and shattered the throne of the Bourbons, also reached the shores of her remotest colonies, and proclaimed the redemption of every slave that moved on French soil. Thus does France remember the paternal advice of Lafayette, and atone for the murder of Toussaint. Thanks be to God, the lily is cleansed of the blood that stained it. The nations of the earth will gaze with delight upon its democratic purity, wherever it shall be seen. Whether in the grape-grown valleys where it first bloomed, or in the Isles of Bouron, Guadeloupe, Martinique, or in Guiana.* The colored people of St. Bartholomews, who were emancipated by a decree of the King of Sweden last year, have lately sent an address to their Liberator. Haiti, by the heroism of her Oge, Toussaint L'Ouverture, Dessalines, Christophe, Petion, and Boyer, have driven the demon of slavery from that island, and have buried his carcass in the sea.

Briefly, and imperfectly have I noticed the former condition of the colored race. Let us turn for a moment to survey our present state. The woeful volume of our history as it now lies open to the world, is written with tears and bound in blood. As I trace it my eyes ache and my heart is filled with grief. No other people have suffered so much, and none have been more innocent. If I might apostrophize, that bleeding country I would say, O Africa! thou has bled, freely bled, at every pore! Thy sorrow has been mocked, and thy grief has not been heeded. Thy children are scattered over the whole earth, and the great nations

---

* The whole number of slaves in the French Colonies were almost 300,000.

have been enriched by them. The wild beasts of thy forests are treated with more mercy than they. The Lybian lion and the fierce tiger are caged to gratify the curiosity of men, and the keeper's hands are not laid heavily upon them. But thy children are tortured, taunted, and hurried out of life by unprecedented cruelty. Brave men formed in the divinest mould, are bartered, sold and mortgaged. Stripped of every sacred right, they are scourged if they affirm that they belong to God. Women sustaining the dear relation of mothers, are yoked with the horned cattle to till the soil, and their heart strings are torn to pieces by cruel separations from their children. Our sisters ever manifesting the purest kindness, whether in the wilderness of their father-land, or amid the sorrows of the middle passage, or in crowded cities, are unprotected from the lusts of tyrants. They have a regard for virtue, and they possess a sense of honor, but there is no respect paid to these jewels of noble character. Driven into unwilling concubinage, their offspring are sold by their Anglo Saxon fathers. To them the marriage institution is but a name, for their despoilers break down the hymeneal altar and scatter its sacred ashes on the winds.

Our young men are brutalized in intellect, and their manly energies are chilled by the frosts of slavery. Sometimes they are called to witness the agonies of the mothers who bore them writhing under the lash, and as if to fill up to overflowing the already full cup of demonism, they are sometimes compelled to apply the lash with their own hands. Hell itself cannot overmatch a deed like this,— and dark damnation shudders as it sinks into its bosom, and seeks to hide itself from the indignant eye of God.

> They till oppression's soil where men,
>   For liberty have bled,
> And the eagle wing of freedom waves,
>   In mockery over head.
> The earth is filled with the triumph shouts
>   Of men who have burst their chains,

But theirs the heaviest of them all
Still lay on their burning veins.

In the tyrants' halls there are luxury,
And wealth, and mental light,
But the very book of the Christian law,
Is hidden from their sight.
In the tyrants' halls there are wine, and mirth,
And songs for the newly free,
But their own low cabins are desolate,
Of all but misery.

Spain, who gave the first impulse and royal sanction to the slave trade, still clings to her idolatry. It rests as a plague spot upon the faces of her people. A case lately ordered before the United States Supreme Court, by one of her subjects, and favored by President Van Buren, secured one of the most important decisions ever given in this Nation. I allude to the case of the *Amistad*, whose whole cargo of souls were emancipated on the high seas, by the heroism of the chieftain, Joseph Cinque. He arose in the strength of his manhood, and slew the captain, and imprisoned the crew, as they were pursuing their course from Havana to Matanzas. Being unacquainted with navigation, he commanded the seamen to steer towards the sun-rise, knowing that his native country was in the East. But the sky becoming cloudy, the traders directed the vessel towards the American coast, expecting to find favor and assistance from their fellow bandits and brother pirates in this country. But in this they were mistaken, for justice triumphed. When the woe-freighted bark neared our coast, and Cinque saw the star-spangled banner floating in the breeze, it was then that the hero addressed his despairing comrades, while a triumphant smile played upon his face, and said, *"Brothers, we would have conquered, but the sea was against us."* A sentence more heroic was never uttered by an untutored savage.

It may be asked why did he despair when he saw the

flag of our country? Here is the answer, and be not surprised at it. Because he had seen it waving protectively from the masts of slavers, when freedom owned him as her child, and when he breathed her spirit on his native hills.

The slave trade is carried on briskly in the beautiful island of Cuba. A few years ago, I witnessed the landing of a cargo of slaves, fresh from the coast of Africa, in the port of Havana, in the presence of the Governor, and under the shadow of the Moro Castle, one of the strongest fortifications of the world.

Recently, a great sacrifice has been made in that Island to the Spirit of despotism, in the death of the Patriot and Poet, Placido. Freedom mourns over his early tomb. The waves of the Atlantic, of whose vastness and sublimity he had sung, chanted his dirge as the tyrants hid him in the grave! Placido was a mulatto, a true Poet, and of course a Patriot. His noble soul was moved with pity as he saw his fellow men in chains. Born to feel, and to act, he made a bold attempt to effect a revolution, and failing in it, he fell a martyr to his principles.

On the day previous to his death, he wrote the following lines, of which Coleridge or Montgomery would not have been ashamed. They present a blaze of poetic fire, intense and sublime: —

O Liberty! I wait for thee,
To break this chain, and dungeon bar;
I hear thy voice calling me,
Deep in the frozen North, afar,
With voice like God's, and vision like a star.

Long cradled in the mountain wind,
Thy mates, the eagle and the storm
Arise; and from thy brow unbind
The wreath that gives its starry form,
And smite the strength, that would thy strength deform.

Yet Liberty! thy dawning light,
Obscured by dungeon bars, shall cast
A splendor on the breaking night,
And tyrants flying thick and fast,
Shall tremble at thy gaze, and stand aghast.

The next day they led Placido forth to execution, and from the mouths of bristling musketry a shower of lead was poured upon his quivering heart. That heart stood still,—and a truer, braver one, never beat in the breast of a mortal man!

The Brazilian Government holds three millions of the colored race in slavery. The United States have about the same number. The Spanish Colonies have one million.

But it is proper to turn the other side of the picture, and I rejoice that there is another side. Nine hundred thousand of these people are enjoying their freedom in the British West India Isles. There are six hundred thousand free people in the United States, while in Haiti we have an independent population of nearly a million. Possessing a land of unsurpassed fertility, they have but to turn their attention manfully to Agricultural pursuits and it will shine forth the brightest Isle that slumbers in the arms of old ocean.

In regard to the enslavement of our race, this Country presents as mournful a picture as any other beneath the sun; but still it is not hopelessly enshrouded in darkness. The good institutions of the land are well adapted to the development of the mind. So far as the oppressed shall make their own way towards them, and shall escape the influence of those that are evil, so far shall they succeed in throwing off their bitter thraldom, and in wrenching the scourge from the hands of tyranny.

Slavery has done much to ruin us, and we ourselves have done some things which effect the same. Perhaps the evils of which I am about to speak arise from slavery, and are the things without which the system cannot exist. But nevertheless we must contribute largely towards their ovcrthrow. If it is in our power to destroy these evils, and we do not, then much of our own blood will be found on us.

We are divided by party feuds, and are torn in pieces by dissensions. Some men have prostituted good talents, for the base purpose of kindling the fires of discord. Some who officiated in the temples said to be dedicated to God, are idolaters to sectarianism. And some too would draw a line of blood distinction, and would form factions upon the shallow basis of complexion. But I am glad to know that the number of this class is small, and small as it is, I pray that we may soon be able to write a cypher in its place. Let there be no strife between us, for we are brethren, and we must rise or fall together. How unprofitable it is for us to spend our golden moments in long and solemn debate upon the questions whether we shall be called, *"Africans" "Colored Americans,"* or *"Africo Americans,"* or *"Blacks."* The question should be, my friends, *shall we arise and act like men, and cast off this terrible yoke?* Many are too apt to follow after shams, and to neglect that which is solid. Thousands are often expended for an hour's display of utter emptiness, which ought to be laid aside to increase our wealth, and for the acquirement of knowledge, and for the promotion of education. Societies, called benevolent, frequently squander more money for the purchase of banners and bandages, and in feasting, than they use in acts of charity. What are regalia and other trappings worth, if they signify nothing but sham and parade? In 1846, $5000 were paid by the oppressed Colored people at the Temperance Celebration held in Poughkeepsie, N.Y., and yet we do not adequately support a single Newspaper in the United States.

The first of August meeting, held in Canandaigua, in 1817, cost the same class not less than $10,000; and yet we do not find *a hundred* of our young men and women in our high-schools and colleges. The gorgeous pageant of the Odd Fellows in October 1817, drew from the pockets of the people, at a very moderate calculation, the sum of

$8000, while many of their offspring who ought to be drinking at the fountain of learning, are mourning by the turbid and cold waters of servile employments. The Free and Accepted Masons can boast nothing over other fraternities in regard to unnecessary expenditures. The Masons have led off in this course of wastefulness, and a majority of the other institutions are but children of the great original, and they resemble their parent more or less. Let no one say that I seek the destruction of these institutions. I desire rather to remove the unfruitful branches of the trees, that it may be ascertained whether their trunks are capable of bearing good fruit. If they can produce good, if there is life in the stock, let them remain that they may be beautified by the dresser's hands. But if the roots are corrupt, and their branches cast a deadly shade, let them be cut down, for why should they cumber the ground?

May God grant, that we may betake ourselves to greater wisdom and frugality. I know that the oppressed above all other people need holidays, and pastimes, but in no case should we bid adieu to our common sense. Let all be careful, lest in this age of ribbon, velvet and gold lace revival, that we do not fall into fanaticism. Fanatics sometimes have strange visions, and it would be strange, "passing strange," should any considerable portion of a whole race imagine themselves in a world of ribbons, painted sticks, and vanity without measure.

We ought to have our monster meetings, but we should assemble with the same spirit, that animated the Irish people, when they were led by that giant of freedom Daniel O'Connell, which should be, to use his own words, to "agitate, and agitate, and agitate until the chains of the three millions are broken." A half penny's worth of green ribbon and a sprig of shamrock signified to the Irishman more than all the gaudy trappings of a Grand Master, or a Prince of Jerusalem. These little things represented a grand principle to the minds of the unconquerable sons of

Erin. *The principles of progress in the ways of truth, and resistance to tyranny should be the bases of all our public demonstrations, and numerical representations.*

We should have likewise, days of bitter bread, and tabernacles in the wilderness, in which to remember our grief-worn brothers and sisters. They are now pleading with a million tongues against those who have despoiled them. They cry from gory fields—from pestilential rice swamps —from cane breaks, and forests—from plantations of cotton and tobacco—from the dark holds of slave ships, and from countless acres where the sugar cane, nods to the sighing winds. They lift up their voices from all the land over which the flag of our country floats. From the banks of our silver streams, and broad rivers, from our valleys and sloping hills, and mountain tops!

The silence that reigns in the region where the pale nations of the earth slumber, is solemn, and awful. But what think ye, when you are told that every rood of land in this Union is the grave of a murdered man, and their epitaphs are written upon the monuments of the nation's wealth. Ye destroyers of my people draw near, and read the mournful inscription; aye! read it, until it is daguerreotyped on your souls. "You have slain us all the day long— you have had no mercy." Legions of haggard ghosts stalk through the land. Behold! see, they come: Oh what myriads! Hark! hear their broken bones as they clatter together! With deep unearthly voices they cry, "We come, we come! for vengeance we come! Tremble, guilty nation, for the God of Justice lives and reigns." The screaming of the eagle as he darts through lightning and storm is unheard because of these voices. The tocsin of the Sabbath, and the solemn organ are mocked by them. They drown the preacher's voice, and produce discord in the sacred choirs. Sworn senators and perjured demagogues, as they officiate around the altar of Moloch in the national capitol, they hear the wailings of the victims of base born democracy, and they are ill at ease in their unexampled hypocrisy.

The father of waters, may roar in his progress to the ocean—the Niagara may thunder, but these voices from the living and the dead, rise above them all.

Such, ladies and gentlemen, are the outlines of the picture of the Colored Race throughout the world. Behind us and on either side are waste places, and deserts, but before us are green spots and living springs.

The genius of slavery in this country has taken his course southward. It has passed its Rubicon, the far distant Sabine. Infatuated with its victories, it has pressed forward to the sandy shores of the Nueces, where it paused but for a moment. It has Texas and moves on beyond the Rio del Norte.

Six slave states added at a breath! one flourish of a pen,
And fetters are riveted on millions more of men,
How all the damned leap up, and half forget their fire,
To think men take such pains to claim the notice of God's
    ire.

Nor has it been satisfied when all this was done. It has laid its hands upon the nation's standard, and has urged its way through flood, and field, until that blood-stained banner waves on the halls of the Montezumas. It claims its victories on the ensanguined plains of Monterrey, Cerro Gordo, Chapultepec, Churubusco, and Buena Vista, and hangs out its stiffened and gory garments from the old grey walls of Vera Cruz. These are but a part of slavery's conquests on this continent. It is among the things that are possible that these triumphs are defeats in disguise. "God taketh the wise in their own craftiness, and the counsel of the ungodly carries headlong." I would not despair of the triumph of freedom in the hemisphere, were Mexico to be annexed to this union. For one I would welcome my dark-browed and liberty-loving brethren to our embrace. Aye! let them come with the population of seven and a half millions. One fifth of that number are white, and they are ultra Abolitionists. Two fifths are Indians, and the other two fifths are of the black, and mixed races. I repeat it, I should not despair if they should come.

The dominions of slavery are directly between Northern and Southern freedom—between Eastern and Western Democracy. In the East the sons of New England are waking up at freedom's call, among the tombs of their fathers.

Grey Plymouth's Rock hath yet a tongue, and Concord is
   not dumb.

The men of the North begin to appreciate the doctrine which has been long inculcated, that in order to be free themselves, they must emancipate the bondmen. The young lion of the West has torn the net of voluntary servitude, and gives signs of his latent strength. "The peculiar Institution" is doomed. President Polk sees this, and he spares neither blood, nor treasure to save it. Mr. John C. Calhoun is aware of it, and like some mighty Colossus, he stands astride the dark and troubled waters of his daring system, and like a frightened girl, appeals piteously to his brethren of the North and the South, to come to the rescue, and save him from a humiliating downfall. His predicament is pictured, very correctly by the gifted and devoted Bard of Liberty, John Greenleaf Whittier.

Where's now the boast, which even thy guarded tongue,
Cold, calm, and proud, in the teeth o' the senate flung,
O'er the fulfillment of thy baleful plan,
Like Satan's triumph, at the fall of man?
How stood'st thou then, thy foot on Freedom planting,
And pointing to the lurid heaven afar,
Whence all could see through the south window's slanting,
Crimson as blood, the beams of the Lone star:
The Fates are just; they give us but our own;
Nemesis ripens what our hands have sown.
There is an eastern story, not unknown,
Doubtless to thee, of one whose magic skill,

Called demons up his water jars to fill;
Deftly, and silently they did his will,
But when the task was done kept pouring still.
In vain with spell and charm the wizard wrought,
Faster and faster were the buckets brought,
Higher, and higher rose the flood around,
Till the fiends clapped their hands above their master
  drowned.

New and startling scenes are passing before us continually. No man of common sense, will declare to-day, that he will not be on the side of freedom to-morrow. All the while the Colored race, are increasing in a ratio unprecedented in the history of any oppressed people.

The Spaniard conquered Mexico three hundred years ago. His impress is scarcely perceptible upon it. Many of the chiefs of the country are mixed blood, some of them pure Indian, while the population, as a whole, is altogether mongrel.

But there is another race (the negro) parallel, corelative, and inter-mixed with the Anglo-American. Include Texas, and go from the East boundary of the Louisiana purchase, to the Rio Grande, thus:

Colored Race	1820	1830	1845
Louisiana	79,500	124,000	245,000
Missouri	10,550	27,000	71,851
Arkansas	1,677	5,000	40,000
Texas	0,000	5,000	50,000
Total	91,727	161,000	406,851

The slaves keep pace with the whites! If carried into Mexico, their masters bring a colored race, and find one there! The oppressive burdens of slavery, therefore, will keep down Anglo-American progress in that direction!

Cincinnati Chronicle

Who is there, after looking at these facts, will question the probability of the assumption, that this republic, and this continent, are to be the theatre in which the grand drama of our triumphant Destiny is to be enacted.

The Red men of North America are retreating from the approach of the white man. They have fallen like trees on the ground in which they first took root, and on the soil which their foliage once shaded. But the Colored race, although they have been transplanted in a foreign land, have clung to and grown with their oppressors, as the wild ivy entwines around the trees of the forest, nor can they be torn thence. At this moment when so much feigned hatred is manifested toward us, our blood is mixed with every tribe from Cape Horn to the Frozen Ocean. Skillful men have set themselves to work at analyzation, and yet in many cases they are perplexed in deciding where to draw the line between the Negro and the Anglo Saxon. Whatever our colorless brethren say of themselves, so far do they proclaim our future position. Do they say in proud exultation,

> No pent up Utica contracts our powers,
> The whole boundless continent is ours,

in this they bespeak our destiny.

There are those who, either from good or evil motives, plead for the utopian plan of the Colonization of a whole race to the shores of Africa. We are now colonized. We are planted here, and we cannot as a whole people, be re-colonized back to our fatherland. It is too late to make a successful attempt to separate the black and white people in the New World. They love one another too much to endure a separation. Where one is, there will the other be also. Ruth, of the Old Testament, puts the resolve of our destiny in our mouths, which we will repeat to those who would expatriate us: "Entreat me not to leave thee nor return from following after thee, for whither thou goest I will go, and where thou lodgest I will lodge; thy people

shall be my people, and thy God shall be my God. Where
thou diest there will I die, and there will I be buried. The
Lord do so to me, and more; if aught but death part thee
and me."

*This western world is destined to be filled with a mixed
race.* Statesmen, distinguished for their forecast, have
gravely said that the blacks must either be removed, or
such as I have stated will be the result. It is a stubborn
fact, that it is impossible to separate the pale man and the
man of color, and therefore the result which to them is
so fearful, is inevitable. All this the wiser portion of the
Colonizationists see, and they labor to hinder it. It matters
not whether we abhor or desire such a consummation, it
is now too late to change the decree of nature and circumstances. As well might we attempt to shake the
Alleghenies with our hands, or to burst the rock of Gibral-
tar with our fists. If the colored people should all consent
to leave this country, on the day of their departure there
would be sore lamentations, the like of which the world
has not heard since Rachel wept for her children, and
would not be comforted, because they were not. We would
insist upon taking all who have our generous and prolific
blood in their veins. In such an event, the American church
and state would be bereaved. The Reverend Francis L.
Hawks, D.D., of the Protestant Episcopal Church, a man
who is receiving the largest salary of any divine in the
country, would be called upon to make the sacrifice of
leaving a good living, and to share the fate of his brethren
according to the flesh. The Reverend Dr. Murphy, of Her-
kimer, N.Y., a Presbyterian, would be compelled to leave
his beloved flock; and how could they endure the loss of a
shepherd so eloquent, so faithful and so kind. We should
be burdened with that *renegade negro* of the United States
Senate, Mr. Yulee, of Florida. We should take *one* of the
wives of Senator Samuel Houston. The consort,—the beautiful Cleopatra of his Excellency, R. M. Johnson, late
Democratic Vice-President of this great nation,—would be
the foremost in the vast company of exiles. After all we

should return to tread the golden sands of Africa, whether we would add to the morality of our kindred across the deep waters future generations would decide. One thing I am certain of, and that is, many of the slaveholders and lynchers of the South are not very moral now. Our cousins of the tribe of Shem are welcome to our deserters. If they are enriched by them they may be assured that we are not impoverished.

On the other continent, the destiny of the colored people will be similar to that of the people among whom they are scattered. Colorphobia is confined almost entirely to the United States and the Canadas. We speak of prejudice against color, but in fact, nothing of the kind exists. The prejudice is against the condition alone. Were not this the case the American feeling would pervade the whole earth.

Many things that were intended for evil to us, will result, I trust, in good. The tyrants have debarred us from the wealth accruing from trade and commerce. This is an evil. But may it not be hoped that we are their juniors in the art of cheating? We have among us some arrant cheats, but it is presumed that but a few will doubt that our white brothers bear off the palm in this department of human depravity. The besetting sins of the Anglo Saxon race are, the love of gain and the love of power. In many instances, while our services could be dispensed with, we have not been permitted to join the army, and of course have not been killed in the wars. We have been driven from the sanctuaries where our oppressors worship, and it may be that we are not quite as hypocritical as their practices have made them. When the great national account shall be rendered before the tribunal of justice, the guilt of course must be borne by those who might have had, or who have used the power of the government. There may, therefore, be some good that may come out of this evil. But no thanks to the evil doers. Their works are evil still, the good comes in spite of them.

The old doctrine of the natural inferiority of the colored race, propagated in America by Mr. Thomas Jefferson, has long since been refuted by Dr. John Mason Goode, and numerous respectable witnesses from among the slandered, both living and dead: Pushkin in Russia, Dumas in France, Toussaint in Haiti, Banaker, Theodore Sedgwick Wright, and a host in America, and a brilliant galaxy in Ancient History.

There are blessings in store for our patient, suffering race,—there is light and glory. The star of our hope is slowly and steadily rising above the horizon. As a land that has long been covered by storm and clouds, and shaken by the thunder, when the storms and clouds had passed away, and the thunder was succeeded by a calm, like that which cheered the first glad morning, and flower and shrub smiled as they looked up to God, and the mountains, plains and valleys rung with joy,—so shall this race come forth and re-occupy their station of renown.

But how shall we hasten on that period? How shall we acquit ourselves on the field where the great battle is to be fought? By following after peace and temperance, industry and frugality, and love to God, and to all men, and by resisting tyranny in the name of Eternal Justice. We must also become acquainted with the arts and sciences, and agricultural pursuits. These will elevate any people and sever any chain.

We must also cherish and maintain a national and patriotic sentiment and attachment. Some people of color say that they have no home, no country. I am not among that number. It is empty declamation. It is unwise. It is not logical—it is false. Of all the people in this wide earth, among the countless hordes of misery, there is not one so poor as to be without a home and a country. America is my home, my country, and I have no other. I love whatever of good there may be in her institutions. I hate her sins. I loathe her slavery, and I pray Heaven that ere long she may wash away her guilt in tears of repentance. I love the green-hills which my eyes first beheld in my infancy. I love every inch of soil which my feet pressed in my youth, and I mourn because the accursed shade of slavery rests upon it. I love my country's flag, and I hope that soon it will be cleansed of its stains, and be hailed by all nations as the emblem of freedom and independence.

8.

SPEECH DELIVERED AT COOPER'S INSTITUTE, NEW YORK CITY, 1860

We have among us men of talent and learning, but such is the prejudice against our race that they are not employed. The African Civilization Society proposes by the assistance of God to aid in the removal of those un-Christian barriers which are placed in the way of our race, by discovering fields for the full and free exercise of their talents and energies either in our own native land, in Central America, in Haiti, in any of the free West Indies Islands, or in Africa the land of our forefathers. We believe that Africa is to be redeemed by Christian civilization and that the great work is to be chiefly achieved by the free and voluntary emigration of enterprising colored people. We hold it to be the duty of the Christians and philanthropists in America, either to send or carry the gospel and civilization into Africa, to thus make some atonement for the wrong and crimes which the people of this country perpetrated upon that injured country. In our efforts to accomplish this work we offer no excuse for the unjust prejudices which exist towards us as a people. We reject the idea, entertained by many, that the black man can never enjoy equal privileges in this country with other classes. To admit this would be to distrust the power of the Gospel, and to doubt its universal triumph. We regard the enslavement of our race to be the highest crime against God and man, and we hope by teaching the Kings and Chiefs of Africa better things to induce them to exterminate the slave-trade and engage in lawful commerce, and in this way aid in destroying slavery in this and all other lands. In carrying out our objects we ask for volunteers and only for volunteers. We appeal to all on the broad grounds of humanity and Christian love. Our plan of operation in Africa is this:

1. To confirm the friendly relations already established by members of the society now there, with some of the chiefs in the Yoruba country, by sending out a company of virtuous, intelligent and enterprising colored people, who are now ready to act as pioneers, and who will proceed as soon as the necessary funds are raised.

2. To purchase lands at suitable points for the use of settlers to be given to them in equal limited quantities and to furnish the necessary mechanical and agricultural implements.

3. To erect school houses and houses of religious worship, to instruct the natives in the arts and sciences, and develop intelligence and industry, the natural resources of the country.

4. To promote lawful commerce upon the coast of Africa, and the growth of cotton and other tropical products by free labor.

With the blessing of God we hope to secure, as the result of our efforts, the diffusion of the Gospel in Africa, and the consequent overthrow of idolatry and superstition, the destruction of the African slave-trade, and the establishment of civil government by free colored men based upon true Christian principles, where ample scope may be afforded to all for the exercise of every mental and moral faculty.

In behalf of this important enterprise, we appeal to the patriot, the philanthropist and the Christian—believing that the generous sympathy of our nature will lead very many to act the part of the good Samaritan towards Africa, by contributing liberally to this object, and thus enabling the society to enter at once upon the work of African evangelization and civilization.

From the accounts recently received from the missionaries and explorers now in the field, the society is encouraged to commence a Christian industrial settlement in Yoruba, where the chiefs are willing to receive missionaries and settlers, and have proffered their friendship to do them good.

The society desires to raise $6,000 to enable this company, with their associates, to enter upon their work in Africa, and earnestly appeal to the friends of the African race for the needed amount, so that the enterprise may be speedily commenced.

I am happy to state that we last week received from our commissioners in Yoruba information that they had succeeded in effecting a treaty with the chiefs of that country for a large and sufficient tract of land, and that they are permitted to form their own municipal laws, subject only to the common law of that country. It is stated that the chiefs and kings are not only willing but anxious to have any number of intelligent colored men of this country, meet with them and settle there. Our plan is not to subvert the government and overthrow the reigning powers of those countries where in the providence of God we may be cast. We believe it would be preferable to sit down by their side, and not only teach the people by precept those principles which we desire them to cherish, but also to teach them by the power of example those things that will elevate their manhood and exalt their nature; and to make them feel that we are a part of themselves—interested in everything which promises to promote their happiness and increase their prosperity. I would state again, that we have now a number of men, of the proper sort, who are willing to embark in this glorious enterprise and who believe as I do, and as the officers and friends of this society believe, that there is a glorious future before Africa. We feel encouraged when we remember that Africa is one of the few countries whose future destiny is a subject of Divine prophecy, of which the Scriptures say, "Ethiopia shall soon stretch out her hands to God, and princes shall come out of Egypt."

9.

EULOGY OF JOHN BROWN, NEW YORK CITY, 1859

Christian Friends and Fellow Countrymen:

The day has come in which the nation is about to suffer a great crime to be perpetrated against the cause of liberty. Today John Brown is to offer up his life a sacrifice for the sake of justice and equal human rights. Henceforth the Second day of December will be called "Martyr's Day." I am not a man of blood. I hold human life to be sacred, and would spare even a man-stealer, if he stood not in the bondman's path to freedom. Often have I indulged the hope of seeing slavery abolished without the shedding of blood; but that hope is clouded. In the signs of the times, I see the dreadful truth, written as by the finger of Jehovah—"For the sins of this nation there is no atonement without the shedding of blood." If it must come O God! prepare us to meet it. The nation needed to see a picture of the future of slavery and its ends and methinks God has been pleased to draw it in crimson lines. Americans, Patriots, Christians, Tyrants, look upon it, and be instructed. Is it not a singular coincidence that in Virginia, the very soil on which African slavery in this part of the New World commenced its reign of terror, the system should receive its first damaging blow? They may murder John Brown, but the blow is struck, and the slave power feels the shock. His work is done, and God's purposes in him are executed, and the divine voice bids him to come up higher. When he dies, he will leave behind him no greater apostle of liberty in all the land. His name and glorious deed shall be cherished by the good and brave, and his widow and fatherless children shall be adopted by the whole army of the Sons of Freedom. Tyrants and despots will everywhere upbraid us for indicting so ghastly a wound on the fair brow of liberty, in a land nick-named the "Model Republic." The withered hand of an old man, whose hairs are white with the frosts of nearly seventy winters, has given the death-blow to American slavery. His heroic deeds will be inscribed on marble, and his grave will be visited by troops of pilgrims. Virginia will be famed in history for having been the home of Washington and the theatre of John Brown's cowardly execution. Farewell brave old man! God be with thee. Steal forth from the scaffold, which cannot dishonor thy name or tarnish thy glory, into the chariot of fire that awaits thee. Go up to meet the army of departed heroes that have gone before thee to the Kingdom of Heaven. Go, and with joy receive thy martyr's crown, which the Lord has prepared for thee. Succeeding ages will cherish thy memory and do justice to thy deeds of renown; and thy amazing courage will be the fruitful theme of orators and the glowing songs of poets. Hero-martyr, farewell!

10.

DISCOURSE DELIVERED IN THE HOUSE OF REPRE-SENTATIVES, WASHINGTON, D.C., 1865

Matthew xxiii. 4: "For they bind heavy burdens, and grievous to be borne, and lay them on men's shoulders, but they themselves will not move them with one of their fingers."

In this chapter, of which my text is a sentence, the Lord Jesus addressed his disciples, and the multitude that hung spell-bound upon the words that fell from his lips. He admonished them to beware of the religion of the Scribes and Pharisees, which was distinguished for great professions, while it succeeded in urging them to do but a little, or nothing that accorded with the law of righteousness.

In theory they were right; but their practices were inconsistent and wrong. They were learned in the law of Moses, and in the traditions of their fathers, but the principles of righteousness failed to affect their hearts. They knew their duty, but did it not. The demands which they made upon others proved that they themselves knew what things men ought to do. In condemning others they pronounced themselves guilty. They demanded that others should be just, merciful, pure, peaceable, and righteous. But they were unjust, impure, unmerciful—they hated and wronged a portion of their fellow-men, and waged continual war against the government of God.

On other men's shoulders they bound heavy and grievous burdens of duties and obligations. The people groaned beneath the loads which were imposed upon them, and in bitterness of spirit cried out, and filled the land with lamentations. But, with their eyes closed, and their hearts hardened, they heeded not, neither did they care. They regarded it to be but little less than intolerable insult to be asked to bear a small portion of the burdens which they were swift to bind on the shoulders of their fellow-men. With loud voice, and proud and defiant mien, they said these burdens are for them, and not for us. Behold how patiently they bear them. Their shoulders are broad, and adapted to the condition to which we have doomed them. But as for us, it is irksome, even to adjust their burdens, though we see them stagger beneath them.

Such was their conduct in the Church and in the State. We have modern Scribes and Pharisees, who are faithful to their prototypes of ancient times.

With sincere respect and reverence for the instruction, and the warning given by our Lord, and in humble dependence upon him for his assistance, I shall speak this morning of the Scribes and Pharisees of our times who rule the State. In discharging this duty, I shall keep my eyes upon the picture which is painted so faithfully and life-like by the hand of the Saviour.

Allow me to describe them. They are intelligent and well-informed, and can never say, either before an earthly tribunal or at the bar of God, *We knew not of ourselves what was right.* They are acquainted with the principles of the law of nations. They are proficient in the knowledge of Constitutional law. They are teachers of common law, and frame and execute statute law. They acknowledge that there is a just and impartial God, and are not altogether unacquainted with the law of Christian love and kindness. They claim for themselves the broadest freedom. Boastfully they tell us that they have received from the court of heaven the Magna Charta of human rights that was handed down through the clouds, and amid the lightnings of Sinai, and given again by the Son of God on the Mount of Beatitudes, while the glory of the Father shone around him. They tell us that from the Declaration of Independence and the Constitution they have obtained a guaranty of their political freedom, and from the Bible they derive their claim to all the blessings of religious liberty. With just pride they tell us that they are descended from the Pilgrims, who threw themselves upon the bosom of the treacherous sea, and braved storms and tempests, that they might find in a strange land, and among savages, free homes, where they might build their altars that should blaze with acceptable sacrifice unto God. Yes! they boast that their fathers heroically turned away from the precious light of Eastern civilization, and taking their lamps with oil in their vessels, joyfully went forth to illuminate this land, that then dwelt in the darkness of the valley of the shadow of death. With hearts strengthened by faith they spread out their standard to the winds of heaven, near Plymouth rock; and whether it was stiffened in the sleet and frosts of winter, or floated on the breeze of summer, it ever bore the motto, *"Freedom to worship God."*

But others, their fellow-men, equal before the Almighty, and made by him of the same blood, and glowing with immortality, they doom to life-long servitude and chains. Yes, they stand in the most sacred places on earth, and beneath the gaze of the piercing eye of Jehovah, the universal Father of all men, and declare, *"that the best possible condition of the negro is slavery."**

Thus man devotes his brother and destroys;
And more than all, and most to be deplored,

* Speech of Fernando Wood, of New York, in Congress, 1864.

As human nature's broadest, foulest blot,
Chains him, and tasks him, and exacts his sweat
With stripes, that Mercy with bleeding heart,
Weeps to see inflicted on a beast.

In the name of the Triune God I denounce the sentiment as unrighteous beyond measure, and the holy and the just of the whole earth say in regard to it, Anathema-ma-ranatha.

What is slavery? Too well do I know what it is. I will present to you a bird's-eye view of it; and it shall be no fancy picture, but one that is sketched by painful experience. I was born among the cherished institutions of slavery. My earliest recollections of parents, friends, and the home of my childhood are clouded with its wrongs. The first sight that met my eyes was a Christian mother enslaved by professed Christians, but, thank God, now a saint in heaven. The first sounds that startled my ear, and sent a shudder through my soul, were the cracking of the whip, and the clanking of chains. These sad memories mar the beauties of my native shores, and darken all the slave-land, which, but for the reign of despotism, had been a paradise. But those shores are fairer now. The mists have left my native valleys, and the clouds have rolled away from the hills, and Maryland, the unhonored grave of my fathers, is now the free home of their liberated and happier children.

Let us view this demon, which the people have worshiped as a God. Come forth, thou grim monster, that thou mayest be critically examined! There he stands. Behold him, one and all. Its work is to chattelize man; to hold property in human beings. Great God! I would as soon attempt to enslave Gabriel or Michael as to enslave a man made in the image of God, and for whom Christ died. Slavery is snatching man from the high place to which he was lifted by the hand of God, and dragging him down to the level of the brute creation, where he is made to be the companion of the horse and the fellow of the ox.

It tears the crown of glory from his head, and as far as possible obliterates the image of God that is in him. Slavery preys upon man, and man only. A brute cannot be made a slave. Why? Because a brute has not reason, faith, nor an undying spirit, nor conscience. It does not look forward to the future with joy or fear, nor reflect upon the past with satisfaction or regret. But who in this vast assembly, who in all this broad land, will say that the poorest and most unhappy brother in chains and servitude has not every one of these high endowments? Who denies it? Is there one? If so, let him speak. There is not one; no, not one.

But slavery attempts to make a man a brute. It treats him as a beast. Its terrible work is not finished until the ruined victim of its lusts, and pride, and avarice, and hatred, is reduced so low that with tearful eyes and feeble voice he faintly cries, "*I am happy and contented—I love this condition.*"

> Proud Nimrod first the bloody chase began,
> A mighty hunter he; his prey was man.

The caged lion may cease to roar, and try no longer the strength of the bars of his prison, and lie with his head between his mighty paws and snuff the polluted air as though he heeded not. But is he contented? Does he not instinctively long for the freedom of the forest and the plain? Yes, he is a lion still. Our poor and forlorn brother whom thou hast labelled "*slave,*" is also a man. He may be unfortunate, weak, helpless, and despised, and hated, nevertheless he is a man. His God and thine has stamped on his forehead his title to his inalienable rights in characters that can be read by every intelligent being. Pitiless storms of outrage may have beaten upon his defenceless head, and he may have descended through ages of oppression, yet he is a man. God made him such, and his brother cannot unmake him. Woe, woe to him who attempts to commit the accursed crime.

Slavery commenced its dreadful work in kidnapping unoffending men in a foreign and distant land, and in piracy on the seas. The plunderers were not the followers of Mahomet, nor the devotees of Hindooism, nor benighted pagans, nor idolaters, but people called Christians, and thus the ruthless traders in the souls and bodies of men fastened upon Christianity a crime and stain at the sight of which it shudders and shrieks.

It is guilty of the most heinous iniquities ever perpetrated upon helpless women and innocent children. Go to the shores of the land of my forefathers, poor bleeding Africa, which, although she has been bereaved, and robbed for centuries, is nevertheless beloved by all her worthy descendants wherever dispersed. Behold a single scene that there meets your eyes. Turn not away neither from shame, pity, nor indifference, but look and see the beginning of this cherished and petted institution. Behold a hundred youthful mothers seated on the ground, dropping their tears upon the hot sands, and filling the air with their lamentations.

Why do they weep? Ah, Lord God, thou knowest! Their babes have been torn from their bosoms and cast upon the plains to die of hunger, or to be devoured by hyenas or jackals. The little innocents would die on the "Middle Passage," or suffocate between the decks of the floating slave-pen, freighted and packed with unparalleled human woe, and the slavers in mercy have cast them out to perish on their native shores. Such is the beginning, and no less wicked is the end of that system which the Scribes and Pharisees in the Church and the State pronounce to be just, humane, benevolent and Christian. If such are the deeds of mercy wrought by angels, then tell me what works of iniquity there remain for devils to do?

This commerce in human beings has been carried on until three hundred thousand have been dragged from their native land in a single year. While this foreign trade has been pursued, who can calculate the enormities and extent of the domestic traffic which has flourished in every slave State, while the whole country has been open to the hunters of men.

It is the highly concentrated essence of all conceivable wickedness. Theft, robbery, pollution, unbridled passion, incest, cruelty, cold-blooded murder, blasphemy, and defiance of the laws of God. It teaches children to disregard parental authority. It tears down the marriage altar, and tramples its sacred ashes under its feet. It creates and nourishes polygamy. It feeds and pampers its hateful handmaid, prejudice.

It has divided our national councils. It has engendered deadly strife between brethren. It has wasted the treasure of the Commonwealth, and the lives of thousands of brave men, and driven troops of helpless women and children into yawning tombs. It has caused the bloodiest civil war recorded in the book of time. It has shorn this nation of its locks of strength that was rising as a young lion in the Western world. It has offered us as a sacrifice to the jealousy and cupidity of tyrants, despots, and adventurers of foreign countries. It has opened a door through which a usurper, a perjured, but a powerful prince, might stealthily enter and build an empire on the golden borders of our southwestern frontier, and which is but a stepping-stone to further and unlimited conquests on this continent. It has desolated the fairest portions of our land, "until the wolf long since driven back by the march of civilization returns after the lapse of a hundred years and howls amidst its ruins."

It seals up the Bible, and mutilates its sacred truths, and flies into the face of the Almighty, and impiously asks, *"Who art thou that I should obey thee?"* Such are the outlines of this fearful national sin; and yet the condition to which it reduces man, it is affirmed, is the best that can possibly be devised for him.

When inconsistencies similar in character, and no more glaring, passed beneath the eye of the Son of God, no wonder he broke forth in language of vehement denunciation. Ye Scribes, Pharisees, and hypocrites! Ye blind guides! Ye compass sea and land to make one proselyte, and when he is made ye make him twofold more the child of hell than yourselves. Ye are like unto whited sepulchres, which indeed appear beautiful without, but within are full of dead men's bones, and all uncleanness!

Let us here take up the golden rule, and adopt the self-application mode of reasoning to those who hold these erroneous views. Come, gird up thy loins and answer like a man, if thou canst. Is slavery, as it is seen in its origin, continuance, and end the best possible condition for thee? Oh, no! Wilt thou bear that burden on thy shoulders, which thou wouldest lay upon thy fellow-man? No. Wilt thou bear a part of it, or remove a little of its weight with one of thy fingers? The sharp and indignant answer is no, no! Then how, and when, and where, shall we apply to thee the golden rule, which says, *Therefore all things that ye would that others should do to you, do ye even so unto them, for this is the law and the prophets.*

Let us have the testimony of the wise and great of ancient and modern times:

Sages who wrote and warriors who bled.

Plato declared that "Slavery is a system of complete injustice."

Socrates wrote that "Slavery is a system of outrage and robbery."

Cyrus said, "To fight in order not to be a slave is noble."

If Cyrus had lived in our land a few years ago he would have been arrested for using incendiary language, and for inciting servile insurrection, and the royal fanatic would have been hanged on a gallows higher than Haman. But every man is fanatical when his soul is warmed by the generous fires of liberty. Is it then truly noble to fight in order not to be a slave? The Chief Magistrate of the nation, and our rulers, and all truly patriotic men think so; and so think legions of black men, who for a season were scorned and rejected, but who came quickly and cheerfully when they were at last invited, bearing a heavy burden of proscriptions upon their shoulders, and having faith in God, and in their generous fellow-countrymen, they went forth to fight a double battle. The foes of their country were before them, while the enemies of freedom and of their race surrounded them.

Augustine, Constantine, Ignatius, Polycarp, Maximus, and the most illustrious lights of the ancient church denounced the sin of slave-holding.

Thomas Jefferson said at a period of his life, when his judgment was matured, and his experience was ripe, "There is preparing, I hope, under the auspices of heaven, a way for a total emancipation."

The sainted Washington said, near the close of his mortal career, and when the light of eternity was beaming upon him, "It is among my first wishes to see some plan adopted by which slavery in this country shall be abolished by law. I know of but one way by which this can be done, and that is by legislative action, and so far as my vote can go, it shall not be wanting."

The other day, when the light of Liberty streamed through this marble pile, and the hearts of the noble band of patriotic statesmen leaped for joy, and this our national capital shook from foundation to dome with the shouts of a ransomed people, then methinks the spirits of Washington, Jefferson, the Jays, the Adamses, and Franklin, and Lafayette, and Giddings, and Lovejoy, and those of all the mighty, and glorious dead, remembered by history, because they were faithful to truth, justice, and liberty, were hovering over the august assembly. Though unseen by mortal eyes, doubtless they joined the angelic choir, and said, Amen.

Pope Leo X testifies, "That not only does the Christian religion, but nature herself, cry out against a state of slavery."

Patrick Henry said, "We should transmit to posterity our abhorrence of slavery." So also thought the Thirty-eighth Congress.

Lafayette proclaimed these words: "Slavery is a dark spot on the face of the nation." God be praised, that stain will soon be wiped out.

Jonathan Edwards declared "that to hold a man in slavery is to be every day guilty of robbery, or of man stealing."

Rev. Dr. William Ellery Channing, in a *Letter on the Annexation of Texas in* 1837, writes as follows:

"The evil of slavery speaks for itself. To state is to condemn the institution. The choice which every freeman makes of death for his child and for every thing he loves in preference to slavery, shows what it is. The single consideration that by slavery one human being is placed powerless and defenceless in the hands of another to be driven to whatever labor that other may impose, to suffer whatever punishment he may inflict, to live as his tool, the instrument of his pleasure, this is all that is needed to satisfy such as know the human heart and its unfitness for irresponsible power, that of all conditions slavery is the most hostile to the dignity, self-respect, improvement, rights, and happiness of human beings. . . . Every principle of our government and religion condemns slavery. The spirit of our age condemns it. The decree of the civilized world has gone out against it. . . . Is there an age in which a free and Christian people shall deliberately resolve to extend and perpetuate the evil? In so doing we cut ourselves off from the communion of nations; we sink below the civilization of our age; we invite the scorn, indignation, and abhorrence of the world."

Moses, the greatest of all lawgivers and legislators, said, while his face was yet radiant with the light of Sinai: "Whoso stealeth a man, and selleth him, or if he be found in his hand, he shall surely be put to death." The destroying angel has gone forth through this land to execute the fearful penalties of God's broken law.

The Representatives of the nation have bowed with reverence to the Divine edict, and laid the axe at the root of the tree, and thus saved succeeding generations from the guilt of oppression, and from the wrath of God.

Statesmen, Jurists, and Philosophers, most renowned for learning, and most profound in every department of science and literature, have testified against slavery. While oratory has brought its costliest, golden treasures, and laid them on the altar of God and of freedom, it has aimed its fiercest lightning and loudest thunder at the strongholds of tyranny, injustice, and despotism.

From the days of Balak to those of Isaiah and Jeremiah, up to the times of Paul, and through every age of the Christian Church, the sons of thunder have denounced the abominable thing. The heroes who stood in the shining ranks of the hosts of the friends of human progress, from Cicero to Chatham, and Burke, Sharp, Wilberforce, and Thomas Clarkson, and Curran, assaulted the citadel of despotism. The orators and statesmen of our own land, whether they belonged to the past, or to the present age, will live and shine in the annals of history, in proportion as they have dedicated their genius and talents to the defence of Justice and man's God-given rights.

All the poets who live in sacred and profane history have charmed the world with their most enchanting strains, when they have tuned their lyres to the praise of Liberty. When the Muses can no longer decorate her altars with their garlands, then they hang their harps upon the willows and weep.

From Moses to Terrence and Homer, from thence to Milton and Cowper, Thomson and Thomas Campbell, and on to the days of our own bards, our Bryants, Longfellows, Whittiers, Morrises, and Bokers, all have presented their best gifts to the interests and rights of man.

Every good principle, and every great and noble power, have been made the subjects of the inspired verse, and the songs of poets. But who of them has attempted to immortalize slavery? You will search in vain the annals of the world to find an instance. Should any attempt the sacrilegious work, his genius would fall to the earth as if smitten by the lightning of heaven. Should he lift his hand to write a line in its praise, or defence, the ink would freeze on the point of his pen.

Could we array in one line, representatives of all the families of men, beginning with those lowest in the scale of being, and should we put to them the question, Is it right and desirable that you should be reduced to the condition of slaves, to be registered with chattels, to have your persons, and your lives, and the products of your labor, subjected to the will and the interests of others? Is it right and just that the persons of your wives and children should be at the disposal of others, and be yielded to them for the purpose of pampering their lusts and greed of gain? Is it right to lay heavy burdens on other men's shoulders which you would not remove with one of your fingers? From the rude savage and barbarian the negative response would come, increasing in power and significance as it rolled up the line. And when those should reply, whose minds and hearts are illuminated with the highest civilization and with the spirit of Christianity, the answer deep-toned and prolonged would thunder forth, no, no!

With all the moral attributes of God on our side, cheered as we are by the voices of universal human nature,—in view of the best interests of the present and future generations—animated with the noble desire to furnish the nations of the earth with a worthy example, let the verdict of death which has been brought in against slavery, by the Thirty-eighth Congress, be affirmed and executed by the people. Let the gigantic monster perish. Yes, perish now, and perish forever!

> Down let the shrine of Moloch sink,
>   And leave no traces where it stood;
> No longer let its idol drink,
>   His daily cup of human blood.
> But rear another altar there,
>   To truth, and love, and mercy given,

And freedom's gift and freedom's prayer,
Shall call an answer down from heaven.

It is often asked when and where will the demands of the reformers of this and coming ages end? It is a fair question, and I will answer.

When all unjust and heavy burdens shall be removed from every man in the land. When all invidious and proscriptive distinctions shall be blotted out from our laws, whether they be constitutional, statute, or municipal laws. When emancipation shall be followed by enfranchisement, and all men holding allegiance to the government shall enjoy every right of American citizenship. When our brave and gallant soldiers shall have justice done unto them. When the men who endure the sufferings and perils of the battle-field in the defence of their country, and in order to keep our rulers in their places, shall enjoy the well-earned privilege of voting for them. When in the army and navy, and in every legitimate and honorable occupation, promotion shall smile upon merit without the slightest regard to the complexion of a man's face. When there shall be no more class-legislation, and no more trouble concerning the black man and his rights, than there is in regard to other American citizens. When, in every respect, he shall be equal before the law, and shall be left to make his own way in the social walks of life.

We ask, and only ask, that when our poor frail barks are launched on life's ocean—

Bound on a voyage of awful length
And dangers little known,

that, in common with others, we may be furnished with rudder, helm, and sails, and charts, and compass. Give us good pilots to conduct us to the open seas; lift no false lights along the dangerous coasts, and if it shall please God to send us propitious winds, or fearful gales, we shall survive or perish as our energies or neglect shall determine.

We ask no special favors, but we plead for justice. While we scorn unmanly dependence; in the name of God, the universal Father, we demand the right to live, and labor, and to enjoy the fruits of our toil. The good work which God has assigned for the ages to come, will be finished, when our national literature shall be so purified as to reflect a faithful and a just light upon the character and social habits of our race, and the brush, and pencil, and chisel, and Lyre of Art, shall refuse to lend their aid to scoff at the afflictions of the poor, or to caricature, or ridicule a long-suffering people. When caste and prejudice in Christian churches shall be utterly destroyed, and shall be regarded as totally unworthy of Christians, and at variance with the principles of the gospel. When the blessings of the Christian religion, and of sound, religious education, shall be freely offered to all, then, and not till then, shall the effectual labors of God's people and God's instruments cease.

If slavery has been destroyed merely from *necessity*, let every class be enfranchised at the dictation of *justice*. Then we shall have a Constitution that shall be reverenced by all: rulers who shall be honored, and revered, and a Union that shall be sincerely loved by a brave and patriotic people, and which can never be severed.

Great sacrifices have been made by the people; yet, greater still are demanded ere atonement can be made for our national sins. Eternal justice holds heavy mortgages against us, and will require the payment of the last farthing. We have involved ourselves in the sin of unrighteous gain, stimulated by luxury, and pride, and the love of power and oppression; and prosperity and peace can be purchased only by blood, and with tears of repentance. We have paid some of the fearful installments, but there are other heavy obligations to be met.

The great day of the nation's judgment has come, and who shall be able to stand? Even we, whose ancestors have suffered the afflictions which are inseparable from a condition of slavery, for the period of two centuries and a half, now pity our land and weep with those who weep.

Upon the total and complete destruction of this accursed sin depends the safety and perpetuity of our Republic and its excellent institutions.

Let slavery die. It has had a long and fair trial. God himself has pleaded against it. The enlightened nations of the earth have condemned it. Its death warrant is signed by God and man. Do not commute its sentence. Give it no respite, but let it be ignominiously executed.

Honorable Senators and Representatives! illustrious rulers of this great nation! I cannot refrain this day from invoking upon you, in God's name, the blessings of millions who were ready to perish, but to whom a new and better life has been opened by your humanity, justice, and patriotism. You have said, "Let the Constitution of the country be so amended that slavery and involuntary servitude shall no longer exist in the United States, except in punishment for crime." Surely, an act so sublime could not escape Divine notice; and doubtless the deed has been recorded in the archives of heaven. Volumes may be appropriated to your praise and renown in the history of the world. Genius and art may perpetuate the glorious act on canvas and in marble, but certain and more lasting monuments in commemoration of your decision are already erected in the hearts and memories of a grateful people.

The nation has begun its exodus from worse than Egyptian bondage; and I beseech you that you say to the people, "*that they go forward.*" With the assurance of God's favor in all things done in obedience to his righteous will, and guided by day and by night by the pillars of cloud and fire, let us not pause until we have reached the other and safe side of the stormy and crimson sea. Let freemen and patriots mete out complete and equal justice to all men, and thus prove to mankind the superiority of our Democratic, Republican Government.

Favored men, and honored of God as his instruments,

speedily finish the work which he has given you to do. *Emancipate, Enfranchise, Educate, and give the blessings of the gospel to every American citizen.*

Hear ye not how, from all high points of Time,—
    From peak to peak adown the mighty chain
That links the ages—echoing sublime
    A Voice Almighty—leaps one grand refrain.
Wakening the generations with a shout,
And trumpet-call of thunder—Come ye out!

Out from old forms and dead idolatries;
    From fading myths and superstitious dreams:
From Pharisaic rituals and lies,
    And all the bondage of the life that seems!
Out—on the pilgrim path, of heroes trod,
Over earth's wastes, to reach forth after God!

The Lord hath bowed his heaven, and come down!
    Now, in this latter century of time,
Once more his tent is pitched on Sinai's crown!
    Once more in clouds must Faith to meet him climb!
Once more his thunder crashes on our doubt
And fear and sin—"My people! come ye out!"

From false ambitions and base luxuries;
    From puny aims and indolent self-ends;
From cant of faith, and shams of liberties,
    And mist of ill that Truth's pure day-beam bends:
Out, from all darkness of the Egypt-land,
Into my sun-blaze on the desert sand!

               *   *   *

Show us our Aaron, with his rod in flower!
    Our Miriam, with her timbrel-soul in tune!
And call some Joshua, in the Spirit's power,
    To poise our sun of strength at point of noon!

God of our fathers! over sand and sea,
Still keep our struggling footsteps close to thee!*

Then before us a path of prosperity will open, and upon us will descend the mercies and favors of God. Then shall the people of other countries, who are standing tip-toe on the shores of every ocean, earnestly looking to see the end of this amazing conflict, behold a Republic that is sufficiently strong to outlive the ruin and desolations of civil war, having the magnanimity to do justice to the poorest and weakest of her citizens. Thus shall we give to the world the form of a model Republic, founded on the principles of justice, and humanity, and Christianity, in which the burdens of war and the blessings of peace are equally borne and enjoyed by all.

* *Atlantic Monthly,* 1862.

Notes

CHAPTER ONE

1. Eric Williams, *Capitalism & Slavery* (New York: Capricorn Books, 1966), p. 7.

2. Leon Litwak, *North of Slavery* (Chicago: University of Chicago Press, 1961).

3. See Charles C. Andrews, *The History of the New York African Free Schools* (New York: Mahlon Day, 1830).

4. Ibid., pp. 39–40.

5. *Liberator*, July 25, 1835.

6. Alexander Crummell, *Africa and America* (Springfield, Mass.: Willey & Co., 1891), pp. 280–81.

7. Benjamin P. Thomas, *Theodore Weld* (New Brunswick, N.J.: Rutgers University Press, 1950).

8. *Colored American*, September 21, 1839.

9. Arnett G. Lindsay, "The Economic Condition of the Negroes of New York Prior to 1861," *Journal of Negro History* (April 1921), pp. 190–99.

10. *Colored American*, September 2, 1837.

11. Monroe N. Work, "The Life of Charles B. Ray," *Journal of Negro History* (October 1919), pp. 361–71.

12. *Colored American*, September 5 and 12, 1841.

13. William Z. Foster, *The Negro People in American History* (New York: International Publishers, 1954), p. 138.

14. Litwak, *North of Slavery*, p. 122.

15. *Colored American*, May 30, 1840; *National Anti-Slavery Standard*, June 11, 1840.

CHAPTER TWO

1. *Colored American*, October 4, 1837. Similarly, Nathaniel Paul, at a meeting of the Albany Anti-Slavery Society in 1838,

noted that some abolitionists were opposed to slavery, "especially that which is 1,000 or 1,500 miles off but . . . hated even more a man who wears a colored skin." Quoted in Benjamin Quarles, *Black Abolitionists* (New York: Oxford University Press, 1969), p. 47.

2. Jane H. and William H. Pease, "Black Power—The Debate in 1840," *Phylon* (Spring 1968), p. 20.

3. George M. Frederickson, *The Black Image in the White Mind* (New York: Harper & Row, 1971), p. 107.

4. *National Anti-Slavery Standard*, June 18, 1840.

5. Quoted in ibid., July 16, 1840; the quotation was reprinted from the *Colored American*.

6. *National Anti-Slavery Standard*, June 27, 1840.

7. *Colored American*, September 12, 1840.

8. Ibid., December 19, 1840.

9. Ibid.

10. *Colored American*, June 16, 1841.

11. *Colored American*, August 6, 1841.

12. *National Anti-Slavery Standard*, September 11, 1845.

13. Ibid.

14. James McCune Smith, *Sketch of the Life and Labors of Rev. Henry Highland Garnet* (Washington, D.C., 1865), p. 39.

15. *Emancipator and Free American*, March 3, 1842.

16. Ibid.

17. Charles H. Wesley, *Neglected History* (Wilberforce: Central State College Press, 1965), p. 62.

18. Quoted in ibid.

19. Frederick Douglass, *The Life and Times of Frederick Douglass* (New York: Collier Books, 1962), p. 229.

20. *Non-Slaveholder*, August 1, 1848.

21. Smith, *Sketch of the Life of H. H. Garnet*, p. 52.

22. *North Star*, September 15, 1848.

23. Ibid.

24. Ibid., November 9, 1849.

25. Ibid., May 12, 1848.

26. Ibid.

CHAPTER THREE

1. *The Confessions of Nat Turner* (Baltimore: Thomas R. Gray, 1831), p. 7.

2. *Minutes of the National Convention of Colored Citizens, Held at Buffalo, New York, on the 15th, 16th, 17th, 18th, and 19th of August, 1843, for the Purpose of Considering Their Moral and Political Condition as American Citizens* (New York: Piercy and Reed, 1843), p. 7.

3. *Emancipator and Free American,* October 12, 1843.

4. *Minutes,* pp. 12–13.

5. Garnet was repeatedly called upon to justify his address during the convention. At the next day's session he spent an hour and a half outlining the main points of the address. He received strong support from William C. Munro, R. H. Johnson, both delegates from New York, and David Lewis from Ohio. The other fourteen delegates who backed him were Theodore Wright, J. H. Townsend, W. P. McIntire, John Wandall, T. Woodson, James Fountain, Jason Jeffrey, H. W. Johnson, A. Peek, S. Talbot, E. B. Dunlap, U. Lett, R. Banks, and Richard Allen. Later, when a move was made to reconsider the vote, two delegates, J. P. Morris and R. Francis, who had previously voted with the majority against Garnet's address, announced that they wished to change their votes in favor of it.

6. Henry Highland Garnet, *An Address to the Slaves of the United States of America* (Troy, 1848), preface.

7. *Liberator,* September 8, 1843.

8. Ibid.

9. Ibid., December 3, 1843.

10. *North Star,* September 15, 1848.

11. Jane H. and William H. Pease, "Black Power—The Debate in 1840," *Phylon* (Spring 1968), p. 26.

12. Quoted in Phillip Foner, *Frederick Douglass* (New York: Citadel Press, 1964), p. 138.

13. *Liberator,* March 12, 1858.

14. James McCune Smith, *Sketch of the Life and Labors of Rev. Henry Highland Garnet* (Washington, D.C., 1865), p. 29.

15. *National Negro Convention, 1847, Proceedings of the National Convention of Colored People and Their Friends, Held in Troy, N.Y., on 6th, 7th, 8th, and 9th October, 1847* (Troy: J. C. Kneeland & Co., 1847), p. 14.

16. Ibid., p. 17.

17. Ibid., p. 19.

18. *North Star,* January 19, 1849.

CHAPTER FOUR

1. W. E. B. Du Bois, *The Philadelphia Negro* (New York: Schocken Books, 1967), p. 207.

2. William Wells Brown, *Narrative of William W. Brown* (New York, 1847), pp. 83–84.

3. *Emancipator and Free American,* November 11, 1845.

4. Ibid.

5. *North Star,* November 10, 1848.

6. Ibid.

7. Ibid., January 19, 1849.

8. W. E. B. Du Bois, *The Negro Church* (Atlanta: Atlanta University Press, 1903), p. 5.

CHAPTER FIVE

1. Robert S. Fletcher, *History of Oberlin College* (Oberlin: Oberlin College, 1943), p. 287.

2. *Illustrated London News,* September 7, 1850.

3. Ibid.

4. Rev. J. W. Loguen, *As a Slave and as a Freeman. A Narrative of Real Life* (Syracuse, 1859), p. 393.

5. *Impartial Citizen,* quoted in the *Liberator,* October 11, 1850.

6. *Frederick Douglass' Paper,* August 20, 1852.

7. *Impartial Citizen,* October 26, 1850.

8. *Liberator,* May 30, 1851.

9. Ibid.

10. Ibid. Garnet had long had great respect for the struggle of the Irish people. At the national Negro convention in 1843, he had offered the following resolution: "Resolved, That we hail with joy the progress which the people of Ireland are making in the cause of liberty, and tender them our hearty sympathy."

11. Samuel Rhodes to Gerrit Smith, November 21, 1850, Syracuse University.

12. *Frederick Douglass' Paper,* March 11, 1852.

13. Garnet manuscript, n.d., Rhodes House Library.

14. *Frederick Douglass' Paper,* September 2, 1853.

15. Ibid.

16. Ibid.

17. Garnet to L. A. Chomerow, October 2, 1854, Rhodes House Library.

18. Ibid.

19. Garnet correspondence, n.d., Rhodes House Library.

20. Garnet to Gerrit Smith, October 3, 1856, Syracuse University.

CHAPTER SIX

1. *Frederick Douglass' Paper,* December 23, 1853.

2. *North Star,* January 26, 1849.

3. Ibid., March 2, 1849.

4. Ibid., January 26, 1849.

5. Ibid.

6. *Proceedings of the National Emigration Convention of Colored People: Held at Cleveland, Ohio, Aug. 24–26, 1854* (Pittsburgh: A. A. Anderson, 1854).

7. *Speech of H. Ford Douglass in Reply to Mr. J. M. Langston Before the National Emigration Convention.*

8. *North Star,* January 26, 1849.

9. Ibid., March 2, 1849.

10. *Frederick Douglass' Paper,* November 25, 1853. The various opinions on the question of emigration were later published in pamphlet form (*Arguments Pro and Con on the Call for a National Emigration Convention,* 1854). In a rejoinder to William J. Watkins, who opposed emigration, Whitfield wrote in the pamphlet:

> The only just reason to hope for the elevation of an oppressed class, is when they begin to examine the causes of their degradation in the fullest extent, to calculate what measures are necessary to promote their elevation, and then push them forward with all their might. . . . When the oppressed class are but a small minority, scattered through the country and the whole organization of government is in the hands of their enemies, with all its power wielded to crush them . . . [then] Emigration is the only resource.

11. *Frederick Douglass' Paper,* March 6, 1853. Also see the May 1, 1853, edition; Delany again takes Mrs. Stowe to task: "I beg leave to say, that she knows nothing about us, 'the Free Colored people of the United States,' neither does any other white person."

12. Martin R. Delany, *The Condition, Elevation, Emigration and Destiny of the Colored People of the United States, Politically Considered* (Philadelphia: Martin Delany, 1852), p. 45. For an excellent short sketch of Delany's life, see Jessie Fauset, "Rank Imposes Obligation," *Crisis* (November 1926), pp. 9–13.

13. Henry Highland Garnet, *The Past and the Present Condition and the Destiny of the Colored Race: A Discourse Delivered at the Fifteenth Anniversary of the Female Benevolent Society of Troy, N.Y.* (Troy: J. C. Kneeland, 1848), p. 6.

14. Ibid., p. 12.

15. Carter G. Woodson, *Free Negro Owners of Slaves in the United States in 1830* (Washington, D.C.: Association for the Study of Negro Life and History, 1924).

16. E. Franklin Frazier, *Black Bourgeoisie* (New York: Collier Books, 1962), p. 35.

17. Garnet, *Past and Present Condition,* p. 22.

18. Quoted in Victor Ullman, *Martin R. Delany: The Beginnings of Black Nationalism* (Boston: Beacon Press, 1971), p. 214.

19. *Constitution of the African Civilization Society* (New Haven, 1861), p. 2.

20. Ibid.

21. Delany, *The Condition of the Colored People*, p. 213.

22. *Weekly Anglo-African*, September 3, 1859.

23. See Howard Bell's introduction to Martin Delany and Robert Campbell, *Search for a Place* (Ann Arbor: University of Michigan Press, 1969), p. 14.

24. Quoted in Martin Delany, *Official Report of the Niger Valley Exploring Party* (New York: Thomas Hamilton, 1861), p. 17.

25. Ibid., p. 64.

26. Quoted in Dorothy Sterling, *The Making of an Afro-American: Martin Robison Delany, 1812–1885* (New York: Doubleday, 1971), p. 201.

27. *Weekly Anglo-African*, II, January 1861.

28. *Anglo-African Magazine*, January 1859, p. 3.

29. *Liberator*, August 19 and 26, 1859.

30. *Weekly Anglo-African*, September 10, 1859.

31. Ibid. For general background information on the Africa-consciousness movement during this period see Earl Ofari, "The Emergence of Black National Consciousness in America," *Black World* (February 1971), pp. 75–86.

32. *Douglass' Monthly*, February 1859.

33. Ibid., October 1859.

34. Carter G. Woodson and Charles H. Wesley, *The Negro in Our History* (Washington, D.C.: Association for the Study of Negro Life and History, 1922), p. 493.

35. *Weekly Anglo-African*, November 17, 1860.

36. Ibid.

37. *New York Herald*, April 13, 1860.

38. Ibid.

39. Ibid.

40. *Weekly Anglo-African*, December 22, 1860.

41. Ibid., January 12, 1861.

42. Ibid., January 19, 1861.

43. Ibid.

44. Alexander Crummell, *The Relations and Duties of the Free Colored Men in America to Africa* (Hartford, 1861).

45. See Hollis Lynch, *Edward Wilmot Blyden* (New York: Oxford University Press, 1967).

46. Davidson Nicol, ed., *Black Nationalism in Africa* (New York: Africana Publishing Corp., 1969), p. 56.

47. *Weekly Anglo-African*, November 17, 1860.

48. Ronald Robinson and John Gallagher, *Africa and the Victorians* (New York: Anchor Books, 1968), pp. 38–40.

49. James Redpath, ed., *A Guide to Hayti* (Boston: Thayer & Eldridge, 1860), pp. 98–99.

50. Ibid., p. 174.

51. Quoted in Ullman, *Martin R. Delany*, p. 254.
52. Quoted in ibid., p. 266.
53. *Anglo-African Magazine*, November 1859, pp. 365–66.
54. J. Dennis Harris, *A Summer on the Borders of the Caribbean Sea* (New York: A. B. Burdick, 1850), p. 176. For other expressions of sentiment favorable to emigration to the Caribbean see the letters from J. M. Whitfield, Holly, and A. V. Thompson in Carter G. Woodson, *The Mind of the Negro as Reflected in Letters Written During the Crisis, 1800–1860* (Washington, D.C.: Associated Publishers, 1926), pp. 500–04.
55. *Weekly Anglo-African*, April 6, 1861.

CHAPTER SEVEN

1. Eric Foner, *Free Soil, Free Labor, Free Men* (New York: Oxford University Press, 1970), p. 301.
2. *Liberator*, October 1, 1858.
3. Garnet to Gerrit Smith, September 10, 1858, Syracuse University Library.
4. Ibid.
5. For an account of Mammy Pleasant's activities in connection with John Brown, see Helen Holdredge, *Mammy Pleasant* (New York: Putnam, 1953).
6. *Liberator*, December 16, 1859.
7. *Weekly Anglo-African*, December 10, 1859.
8. W. E. B. Du Bois, *John Brown* (New York: International Publishers, 1962), p. 6.
9. *Weekly Anglo-African*, September 24, 1859.
10. Herbert Aptheker, *The American Civil War* (New York: International Publishers, 1961), p. 13.
11. *Douglass' Monthly*, June 1863.
12. Ibid.
13. William Z. Foster, *The Negro People in American History* (New York: International Publishers, 1954), p. 242.
14. James McCune Smith, *Sketch of the Life and Labors of Rev. Henry Highland Garnet* (Washington, D.C.: 1865), p. 61.
15. Ibid., pp. 75–76.
16. Quoted in Jacqueline Bernard, *Journey Toward Freedom* (New York: Dell, 1969), p. 215.
17. *Weekly Anglo-African*, August 21, 1865.
18. Ibid., September 16, 1865.
19. Ibid.
20. Garnet to Gerrit Smith, October 23, 1865, Syracuse University Library.
21. *Weekly Anglo-African*, September 16, 1865.

22. Ibid., August 5, 1865.

23. James S. Allen, *Reconstruction: The Battle for Democracy, 1865–1876* (New York: International Publishers, 1937), p. 48.

24. Garnet to Gerrit Smith, October 23, 1865.

25. *Washington National Republican*, January 31, 1866.

26. August Meier and Elliot Rudwick, *From Plantation to Ghetto* (New York: Hill & Wang, 1966), p. 158.

27. Quoted in "Henry Highland Garnet," Church Historical Series No. 1 (Western Pennsylvania Research and Historical Society, Pittsburgh, n.d.).

28. Garnet correspondence, June 23, 1876, New York Historical Society.

29. Howard Zinn, "American Liberalism, Source of Negro Radicalism," *Boston University Graduate Journal*, Vol. 16, No. 1 (1968).

30. Henry M. Turner, *African Letters* (Nashville: A.M.E. Sunday School Union, 1893), twelfth letter.

Bibliographic Note

While gathering material on Garnet's life, I was sad to discover that most of his private papers, which had been kept by a granddaughter in Florida, were lost in a fire several years ago. This is a serious loss to researchers who plan future work on the black movements of the pre–Civil War decades of the nineteenth century.

A great deal of the information for this study came from abolitionist newspapers and periodicals. Most important were the *Colored American, Weekly Advocate, Freedom's Journal*, the *Impartial Citizen, North Star* (also known as *Fredcrick Douglass' Paper* and *Douglass' Monthly*), the *Emancipator*, the *Liberator, National Anti-Slavery Standard, Weekly Anglo-African*, and the *Anglo-African Magazine*. Others consulted were the *Illustrated London News*, the London *Times*, and the *New York Herald*.

There is a scarcity of material dealing directly with Garnet's life. James McCune Smith's *Sketch of the Life and Labors of Rev. Henry Highland Garnet* is the closest approximation of a biography. Published in 1865, this work concentrates mainly on Garnet's early life. Several books include brief biographical material on Garnet. They are Lerone Bennet's *Pioneers in Protest*, John Cromwell's *The Negro in American History*, Alexander Crummell's *Africa and America*, Carter G. Woodson's essay in the *Dictionary of American Biography*, William Wells Brown's *The Black Man*, William J. Simmons' *Men of Mark*, and William C.

Nell's *The Colored Patriots of the American Revolution*. In addition to these, there are William Brewer's description of his life in the *Journal of Negro History* (January 1928) and an article in Church Historical Series No. 1, published by the Western Pennsylvania Research and Historical Society. Master's theses on Garnet include Ernest Miller's "The Anti-Slavery Role of Henry Highland Garnet" (Union Theological Seminary, 1968–1969) and W. A. Hunton's "What a Negro Preacher Did in 1865" (Howard University, 1925). Scattered information on Garnet can be found in the *Journal of Negro History, Phylon,* and the *Negro History Bulletin.*

Several letters and assorted documents by Garnet are with the Crummell Papers (Schomburg Library), Banneker Papers (Historical Society of Pennsylvania), May Papers (Cornell University), Gerrit Smith Papers (Syracuse University), Andrew Johnson Papers (Library of Congress), Ullman Papers (New York Historical Society).

Hollis Lynch's *Pan-Negro Nationalism in the New World, Before 1862* (Boston University Papers on Africa, Vol. 11, African History, 1966), Howard Bell's *A Survey of the Negro Convention Movement, 1830–1861* (Ph.D. dissertation, Northwestern University, 1953), and Bill McAdoo's "Pre-Civil War Black Nationalism" (*Progressive Labor Magazine,* June–July 1966) are three studies that give valuable insights into the black nationalist movements of the nineteenth century. In particular, McAdoo's piece, written from a Marxist viewpoint, provides a critical interpretation of the trends within the nationalist ideology of the 1850's.

Perhaps the best way to follow the debates over the programs and strategies formulated by blacks during the early decades of the nineteenth century is to check the minutes of the various state and national conventions blacks held. The key national Negro conventions in which Garnet participated were those of 1843, 1847, and 1864. The minutes of each are preserved at the Schomburg Library and in Howard University's Moorland Collection.

I am indebted to Mrs. Jean Hutson and Mrs. Dorothy Porter, respectively, for their assistance here.

The following books provide necessary background material on this historical period: James S. Allen's *Reconstruction: The Battle for Democracy, 1865–1876*, Herbert Aptheker's *A Documentary History of the Negro People in the United States*, Martin R. Delany and Robert Campbell's *Search for a Place: Black Separatism and Africa, 1860*, Howard Brotz's *Negro Social and Political Thought, 1850–1920*, Martin R. Delany's *The Condition, Elevation, Emigration and Destiny of the Colored People of the United States, Politically Considered*, William Z. Foster's *The Negro People in American History*, Henry H. Garnet's *Walker's Appeal/An Address to the Slaves of the United States of America*, James Theodore Holly and J. Dennis Harris' *Black Separatism and the Caribbean, 1860*, Leon Litwak's *North of Slavery*, Hollis Lynch's *Edward Wilmot Blyden*, James McPherson's *The Negro's Civil War*, Benjamin Quarles' *Black Abolitionists*, Victor Ullman's *Martin R. Delany: The Beginnings of Black Nationalism*, Charles H. Wesley's *Neglected History*, and Carter G. Woodson's *The African Background Outlined*.

Index